DEFEATING
the INVISIBLE ENEMY

An ordinary girl's guide to becoming
an autoimmune warrior

DANNI MACPHERSON

Defeating the Invisible Enemy
© Danni Macpherson 2022

All rights reserved. No part of this publication may be reproduced, stored in a retrieval system, or transmitted in any form or by any means, electronic, mechanical, photocopying, recording or otherwise, without the prior written permission of the author.

ISBN: 978-1-922854-40-7 (paperback)
        978-1-922854-41-4 (eBook)

 A catalogue record for this book is available from the National Library of Australia

Printed in Australia by Ocean Reeve Publishing
www.oceanreevepublishing.com
Published by Danni Macpherson and Ocean Reeve Publishing

This book is the reassuring hug that you've been looking for to realise you're not alone on your health journey and that there is hope for you too to heal the right way and avoid the pitfalls of misguided medical treatment.

—Helen Marshall, founder of Primal Alternative

Danni is a true autoimmune warrior and an inspiring example of what can be achieved through courage, determination, and a positive mindset. In the book, Danni opens up about her own personal struggles and how her auto immune condition has impacted her life; every aspect of her life. Her inspiring journey has ignited a passion in her to apply what she has learned, as she now helps others succeed in their own wellness journey.

This book covers everything from functional nutrition to lifestyle and environment to mental health and well-being.

If you are ready to take control of your life, I encourage you to read Danni's book. It is a game changer for those with autoimmune conditions. She offers practical and creative solutions. You won't be disappointed.

—Stacey Hardy, Functional Nutrition Coach, Life Coach, NLP and Timeline Therapy Practitioner, Hypnotherapist

Danni has opened my eyes to a condition of which I had little understanding. I believe everyone with these conditions or any close relation/friend of a sufferer should read this book. I hope and wish that Danni becomes a leading personality in the battle against illness and disease.

—Dr Marc Frochot

First it was gut health, then it was the microbiome followed closely by the gut-brain connection. And now, whilst many health concerns are indeed being linked to the gut, the exact cause of autoimmune disorders, is still relatively unknown. One theory is that some microorganisms (such as bacteria or viruses) or drugs may trigger changes that confuse the immune system. And whilst more research is being carried out, this book 'Defeating the Invisible Enemy' is ahead of its time and trailblazing the what, why, and how of all autoimmune issues. With science, personal stories, and amazing tips, ideas and protocols, this book will support you to healing and living your best life in the best way. This is a must-have for all who have been diagnosed, or questioning if they will be diagnosed, with an autoimmune disease. Cannot recommend it highly enough.

—Kim Morrison, Author, Practitioner, Director, Mentor, Health & Lifestyle Educator

Dedication

*For my parents, who believed in me long before
I believed in myself.
Rest in peace xx*

Disclaimer

This book is intended for reference only, not as a medical manual. The information given here is designed to help you make informed decisions about your health. It is not intended to be a substitute for any treatment that may have been prescribed by your doctor.

Mention of specific companies or individuals in this book does not imply they endorse this book, its author, or publisher.

Contents

Dedication v
Disclaimer vii
Introduction xiii

Section 1: How I Came To Be On This Journey 1
    The Spoon Theory, written by Christine Miserandino 9

Section 2: Autoimmune Disease FAQs 21
    What is an Autoimmune Disease? 23
    What Factors Contribute to Autoimmune Disease? 25
    Genetics 26
    Environment 27
    Trauma 28
    Diet and Exercise 28
    What Is Leaky Gut and What Roles Does it Play in Autoimmune Disease? 32
    How Are Autoimmune Diseases Treated? 33
    Coping with a Diagnosis 35

Section 3: The Autoimmune Warrior Protocol 37
Nutrition 41
'It's Convenient' 43
Elimination or Substitution 45
    Substitutions 46
The Paleo/Keto Approach 49
    Gluten-containing Foods 51
    Sugar 53
    Dairy 56
    Soy 58
    Corn 58

- Grains 60
- Nightshade Vegetables 61
- Alcohol 63
- A Note about Meat 64
- Fermented Food 67
- Bone Broth 69
- Healthy Fats. 70
- Offal (Organ Meat) 71
- Seafood and Shellfish. 72
- Vegetables 73
- A Word About Supplements 73
- An Even Briefer Note about Supplementation to Build Immunity Against Covid 74

What's in My Fridge and Pantry?. 75
Typical Meals Enjoyed in My House. 77
Nutrition Action Steps. 79
- Step 1—Become Aware of What You Are Consuming 79
- Step 2—Make Changes to Create Healthier Habits. 81
- Drink 2–3 Litres of Filtered Water Each Day 83
- Step 3—Supplement to Enhance Healing and Nurturing. 84
- Step 4—Reintroduction 85

Lifestyle and Environment 87
- Stress 88
- Exposure to chemicals—Cleaning Products, Skincare, Pesticides 89
- Exposure to EMFs. 92
- Holistic Therapies. 94
- Additional Therapies I've Researched But Not Yet Tried 96
- Use of Essential Oils. 97

Lifestyle Action Steps 107
- Step 1—Reduce Toxic Load. 107
- Step 2—Rest to Heal 109
- Step 3—Move to Thrive 110
- Step 4—Connect to Mind and Body. .111

Mindset 113
   Manifest 116
   Meditate 119
   Gratitude.. 120
   Give 121
Mindset Action Steps 123
   Step 1—Awaken the Soul........................ 123
   Step 2—Develop Your Spirituality................ 124

Section 4: Healthy Habits for Life 127

Work With Me 129
   Connect with Me................................ 130

Bibliography 131

Recommended Resources 135
   Nutrition 135
   Lifestyle.. 136
   Mindset.. 137

Acknowledgements 139

Introduction

I'm just an average person who has not allowed a diagnosis to define who I am or how I live.

Eleven years ago, when I first heard the words 'autoimmune disease', I had no idea it would lead me down the path of documenting years of pain and the relentless pursuit to heal my body naturally. As you'll learn, I was brought up in the holistic healthcare space and enjoyed learning about health and nutrition at school; however, that was only the beginning of my journey. Since I received my diagnosis, I have sought alternative treatments for my condition. I have studied with The Nutrition Academy, founded by Cyndi O'Meara, a nutritionist with over forty years of experience, learning about the fundamentals of functional nutrition and how to apply these concepts in everyday life. I have recently completed a specialised course delving into the microbiome and have qualified as an Autoimmune Paleo Protocol Certified Coach. You might notice throughout the book that I refer to being an avid bookworm; I have devoured many books on the topic of using food as medicine, which has led me to consider other factors, such as lifestyle and environment, as well. I have listened to many a podcast and watched many interviews with experts from all over the world who talk about the organic makeup of human beings and how our bodies benefit from nature and natural products.

I was asked once what would happen if I didn't write this book and I replied without thinking—'People will remain ill; they will live with their illness without realising there is an alternative, and I don't want anyone to live with daily pain.' Having experienced the pain, stress, and uncertainty of living with a chronic illness, it became my deepest desire to help and support others through their journey, and writing this book became a way to relay my message to more people in one hit. This book details my journey and provides you with the protocol I undertook to overcome my autoimmune condition. While no treatment is a one-size-fits-all approach, this book will broaden your knowledge of chronic illness and the nutrition and lifestyle factors that play a role in illness and disease, as well as various treatment options available. I have included practical tips and actionable steps for you to try for yourself and have provided connection details, should you wish to investigate further with me.

Initially, I focused the content of this book on those battling autoimmune diseases. But as I grow and evolve, I understand that it is not just those suffering a chronic illness that could benefit from my story. Anyone, regardless of where they're at with their health journey, could learn something from this book. It's not just food, movement, and environment that contribute to a healthy disposition; it is also belief. The belief that we can live better. The belief that we can do better. The belief that we can inspire and motivate others. Most importantly, the belief in ourselves. I often said throughout my battle, 'This is the hand I've been dealt; I must play the cards as best I can,' but I understand now I can win every hand. I hope that you will embrace this book with the same vigour, that you will take away what you need for now and revisit it when you need further affirmation. You won't always start on the right foot; I had many false starts before I came to be on the path I'm on now, but I got there, and you will too. It just takes time, commitment, and patience. It is my mission, like that of my mentors, to educate you about the role that nutrition and lifestyle factors play in health, and once you acquire that knowledge, you will share it with others so that together, we can eradicate illness and disease. I look forward to sharing the journey with you.

Section 1:

How I Came To Be On This Journey

The only thing tough enough to kick my butt is me!
— Anon

A few months shy of my thirtieth birthday, a doctor uttered the words 'mixed connective tissue disease' (MCTD) along with 'rare', 'autoimmune disease', and 'unknown prognosis'. I finally had an answer to enduring months of pain and fatigue, the reason for the inflammation throughout my body, an explanation for the 'flares' (as we 'lupies' call it when we experience unpredictable and debilitating bursts of symptoms), the result of becoming a human pin cushion as I endured test after test. I was gutted. To be so young and not understand what an autoimmune condition, let alone MCTD, was or how the diagnosis would affect my body and daily life left me feeling withdrawn and lacking hope. I did not have answers regarding how to manage it, how it would affect me long-term, or how I had even ended up with the condition. Raised by my father, a chiropractor, and my mother, a naturalist, I had what I believed to be a good understanding of the human body and a slight distrust of the medical profession, whose answer, it seemed, was to throw a script at you, effectively placing a bandaid over the issue without ever really getting to the root cause—if medication is the 'cure' to make you feel better, why does it have side effects, and why do you need to be on it for the rest of your life?

Although we lived 500 metres from McDonald's, fast food was not a regular feature in our weekly meals, and we were an active family. At a crossroads after high school, Dad contemplated becoming a PE teacher before settling on chiropractic and traveling to the USA to study at Palmer College. Mum enjoyed playing tennis, so much so that we installed a court in our backyard on which my brother and I undertook private lessons. I played netball while my over-achieving sibling tried his hand at every sport— football, cricket, basketball, soccer, tennis ... anything that involved activity. When we lived in Queensland, we were active swimmers and snorkellers and enjoyed getting out on the jet ski. Oh, and there was the odd occasion where we would rollerblade down to the harbour (although getting back up the hill was rather tiresome).

It seemed incomprehensible that my body was failing me when I had treated it so well! My curiosity was piqued; I needed answers and was ready to venture down the rabbit hole. Unwilling to accept my diagnosis and the doctor's eagerness to medicate, I went about seeking the answers the medical professionals couldn't give; specifically, how do I heal naturally?

The answers came over seven years and a lot of trial and error. And, if I'm honest, there were times when I wasn't always committed (particularly when I was faced with giving up wine!). I came to realise that this issue had been building in my system for twenty-two years since I suffered peritonitis and underwent lifesaving surgery. I didn't know how ill I had been; at only seven years of age, my parents kept those details to themselves, telling me only that my appendix had been removed. I was in my twenties when I learned that my appendix had ruptured and the toxins that were secreted had found their way into my uterus, causing terrible discomfort while poisoning my body; I was less than twenty-four hours from death. This revelation did not surprise me; my hospital admission was the day after my birthday, but I had a party scheduled that I was determined would go ahead, and nobody could talk me out of it, despite me having been extremely unwell in the preceding days. To give you an idea of how much pain I was in on that day, my parents decided to sit me in a cane chair, pillows and cushions fluffed up around me, and when I wanted to move, they would lift the entire chair—it was far less painful than physically touching me. Since that operation, I felt weak and fatigued; I couldn't play a full game of netball without having trouble breathing, as though I were being stabbed in the chest; and my legs felt heavy, as though they were full of lead. I thought that was normal; I thought that kids who didn't feel like that must put in more effort, that they trained harder or slept longer hours to give their body more time to recover (I was also a bit of an insomniac, which is an autoimmune trait). At that age, I never considered there might be an underlying issue, and my parents were probably just happy that I was there, feebly running around, and hadn't died on the operating table.

The onset of my symptoms accelerated after a second lifesaving surgery. The scar tissue from the first operation was wide and hardened across my stomach, and it was strangling my bowel. Gosh, how much more could my body take? In the hospital, pins and needles came quickly. I didn't think much of it at the time, just my body reacting to the surgery and being uncomfortable. I was discharged after a few days, only to be readmitted the same night because I began to vomit. Imagine, if you will, your stomach contracting after you've just undergone surgery; it felt like fire tearing through my body, ripping me open. At the time, I likened the pain to giving birth, although having never experienced labour, I can only imagine it would be at least that painful, except I didn't get to hold a cute baby in my arms at the end. Despite not having thrown up again, I was kept in hospital 'jail' for another three days under observation before being allowed to go home (note to self: sarcastic wit towards the doctors is not tolerated in the light-hearted manner in which it is meant to be taken) with a stern warning not to overexert myself. On that point, I agreed with them; I was incredibly weak and needed time to recover. I allowed myself to rest for a couple of weeks, not giving much consideration to the irritating symptoms that kept occurring; that is, until I went back to work.

At the time, I worked in a fresh seafood shop, preparing stock for display and selling to customers. As the display cabinet was filled with fresh ice, every day, and I was in and out of cool rooms, it was quite a cold position on a normal day for a normal person. Within seconds of entering the cool room, my fingers were frozen, right down to the palms of my hands, all shades of white, pink, and purple. *Must have cut a nerve during the op,* was my thought, as I ran my hands under warm water to no avail; those fingers were frozen for at least half the day. I experienced that battle with my fingers every day. Then I broke out with pimples and a mean, red, inflamed rash on my face (so terrible that a beautician recoiled in shock). *Hmm, probably just my body getting rid of all the drugs they pumped into me,* was my justification. And then things went downhill at a great rate of knots.

I felt more fatigued, I couldn't focus, I began slurring my words (without the help of alcohol), and I would get sentences mixed up as though my brain was working overtime and my mouth couldn't keep up. People began looking at me like I was on crack, or like I was in a permanent state of stroke. I had to forfeit my job as a fishmonger; I just couldn't stand the pain that came with thrusting my hands into icy display cabinets, and so, I returned home to Dad. He was at a loss to explain my symptoms; the pain overwhelmed chiropractic adjustments. *Maybe I just need more time to recover*, I told myself. After all, I had been very unwell. I did what anyone would do when their niggling subconscious is slapping them in the face with an impending issue; I buried my head in the sand. But, of course, the time came when I could no longer ignore the burgeoning health crisis. One morning, I woke feeling things weren't quite right. I couldn't get out of bed, the pain was excruciating, and I felt paralysed; my mind was telling my knees to bend, but my body was not responding. I was feeling every bit of eighty years old, yet still not thirty; what was going on with my body?

I am not ashamed to admit that some dark days followed my diagnosis. Many in my social circle found it difficult to believe I had a problem, as I didn't look sick; I believe the terms used to describe me were 'hypochondriac' and 'drama queen'. My family members were always calling me a drama queen when I was young; I thought it was because I was always singing and dancing, a born entertainer! I was devastated to learn that they thought I was overdramatic and meant it as a criticism (although it is perfect behaviour for actresses, which I had always hoped to be). As a result, I bottled everything up. If I was unwell and experiencing a flare, I wouldn't speak about it. If I needed help around the house because I couldn't lift a washing basket, make a bed, or cook a meal, I wouldn't ask for it. If I needed someone to drive me to appointments because I was in pain or fatigued, I wouldn't ask. That was a very isolating time for me as I managed the best I could. For those of you who feel like your voice is not being heard because you don't look sick, know this—I *hear* you when you say you're in pain, and I *see* you. I know what it takes to get out of bed each day—I became quite adept at the roll, drop, and crawl technique. It would then take the better part of an hour to get some heat into my body and get dressed. Driving to work was another battle, so when people mocked me for not being able to drive a manual, I shared my gratitude for never having owned a car that would bring about more pain. Every movement, every activity and would zap a little more energy from me to the point that by the time I returned home each day, I was exhausted and unable to prepare or even cook a meal. I began to live off frozen meals and bottles of wine, if I could twist the cap off! These were the moments I desperately needed support, but my voice remained silent.

I tried hard to remain upbeat, determined not to let my condition get the better of me, but there's only so much of a beating you can take, physically, before it starts to affect you mentally. I had a partner when I was first diagnosed, but he struggled as he watched me stumbling through the motions of daily life, knowing there was nothing he could do to alleviate the pain. After he left, I wondered if I really wanted to bring someone else into this daily battle. I was independent and stubborn; how could I ask another to join me, knowing that my health could worsen, and therefore, be a hindrance in their life too?

My father was in denial; he refused to believe that I had an autoimmune condition despite his healthcare background and knowing what I had experienced with my two surgeries. Maybe there was also a feeling of guilt; had he been able to put his animosity towards the medical profession aside and taken action at the first sign of trouble, I may never have been near death and may not have developed the ensuing autoimmune condition. For my father, who was a proud man, that would have been a bitter pill to swallow. At night, when I couldn't sleep despite being utterly exhausted, I was on my own with the pain and my thoughts. It was a fraught mental battle. But I had to keep going, put one foot in front of the other and keep moving forward, or, as the Pisces that I am, just keep swimming, swimming, swimming … I was extremely fortunate that I had a very good friend (who was also my boss) who would turn up on my doorstep, every morning, with a coffee and ask how he could help me that day. We would sit in my lounge room and watch *Gossip Girl* (please, no judgement; it was mindless viewing to take my mind off the pain, but I secretly enjoyed it) while I finished doing my make-up and he straightened my hair. It was thanks to him that I discovered how therapeutic bathing could be. He researched tirelessly, almost as much as I, and for that, and his unwavering support, I will be forever grateful.

This particular friend came across a fantastic explanation of what it is like living with chronic illness titled *The Spoon*

Theory by Christine Miserandino;[1] I urge all of you to share this story with the family and friends that don't quite understand what it takes for you to get through each day. Once you've begun the healing process, you'll be able to reread this at various stages and observe how far you've progressed. How many spoons do you now have left at the end of each day as opposed to when you started?

The Spoon Theory, written by Christine Miserandino

My best friend and I were in the diner, talking. As usual, it was very late, and we were eating French fries with gravy. Like normal girls our age, we spent a lot of time in the diner while in college, and most of the time we spent talking about boys, music, or trivial things, that seemed very important at the time. We never got serious about anything in particular and spent most of our time laughing. As I went to take some of my medicine with a snack as I usually did, she watched me with an awkward kind of stare, instead of continuing the conversation. She then asked me out of the blue what it felt like to have Lupus and be sick. I was shocked not only because she asked the random question, but also because I assumed she knew all there was to know about Lupus. She came to the doctors with me, she saw me walk with a

---

[1] The Spoon Theory by Christine Miserandino, reprinted with permission, accessible via https://butyoudontlooksick.com/articles/written-by-christine/the-spoon-theory/?fbclid=IwAR2c6pboxGu65s9jszQk9IO-wtH-VhOC5jdE16SRBC2fcKIiAe9Bwt4mslt0

cane, and throw up in the bathroom. She had seen me cry in pain, what else was there to know? I started to ramble on about pills, and aches and pains, but she kept pursuing, and didn't seem satisfied with my answers. I was a little surprised, as being my roommate in college and friend for years, I thought she already knew the medical definition of Lupus. Then she looked at me with a face every sick person knows well, the face of pure curiosity about something no one healthy can truly understand. She asked what it felt like, not physically, but what it felt like to be me, to be sick. As I tried to gain my composure, I glanced around the table for help or guidance, or at least stall for time to think. I was trying to find the right words. *How do I answer a question I never was able to answer for myself? How do I explain every detail of every day being affected, and give the emotions a sick person goes through with clarity?*

I could have given up, cracked a joke like I usually do, and changed the subject, but I remember thinking if I don't try to explain this, how could I ever expect her to understand. If I can't explain this to my best friend, how could I explain my world to anyone else? I had to at least try. At that moment, the spoon theory was born. I quickly grabbed every spoon on the table; hell, I grabbed spoons off of the other tables. I looked at her in the eyes and said, 'Here you go, you have Lupus.' She looked at me slightly confused, as anyone would when they are being handed a bouquet of spoons. The cold metal spoons clanked in my hands, as I grouped them together and shoved them into her hands. I explained that the difference between being sick and being healthy is having to make choices or to consciously think about things when the rest of the world doesn't have to. The healthy have the luxury of a life without choices, a gift most people take for granted. Most people start the day with an unlimited amount of possibilities, and energy to do whatever they desire, especially young people. For the most part, they do not need to worry about the effects of their actions. So, for my explanation, I used spoons to convey this point. I wanted something for her to actually hold, for me to then take away, since most people who get sick feel a "loss" of a life they once knew. If I was in control of taking away the spoons, then she would know what it feels like to have someone or something else, in this case, Lupus, being in control.

She grabbed the spoons with excitement. She didn't understand what I was doing, but she is always up for a good time, so I guess she thought I was cracking a joke of some kind like I usually do when talking about touchy topics. Little did she know how serious I would become? I asked her to count her spoons. She asked why, and I explained that when you are healthy you expect to have a neverending supply of "spoons". But when you have to now plan your day, you need to know exactly how many "spoons" you are starting with. It doesn't guarantee that you might not lose some along the way, but at least it helps to know where you are starting. She counted out twelve spoons. She laughed and said she wanted more. I said no, and I knew right away that this little game would work, when she looked disappointed, and we hadn't even started yet. I've wanted more "spoons" for years and haven't found a way yet to get more, why should she? I also told her to always be conscious of how many she had, and not to drop them because she can never forget she has Lupus. I asked her to list off the tasks of her day, including the most simple. As, she rattled off daily chores, or just fun things to do; I explained how each one would cost her a spoon. When she jumped right into getting ready for work as her first task of the morning, I cut her off and took away a spoon. I practically jumped down her throat. I said, "No! You don't just get up. You have to crack open your eyes, and then realize you are late. You didn't sleep well the night before. You have to crawl out of bed, and then you have to make yourself something to eat before you can do anything else, because if you don't, you can't take your medicine, and if you don't take your medicine, you might as well give up all your spoons for today and tomorrow too.'

 I quickly took away a spoon and she realized she hasn't even gotten dressed yet. Showering cost her a spoon, just for washing her hair and shaving her legs. Reaching high and low that early in the morning could actually cost more than one spoon, but I figured I would give her a break; I didn't want to scare her right away. Getting dressed was worth another spoon. I stopped her and broke down every task to show her how every little detail needs to be thought about. You cannot simply just throw clothes on when you are sick. I explained that I have to see what clothes I can physically put on; if my hands hurt that day buttons are out of the question. If I have bruises that day, I need to wear long sleeves, and if I have a fever, I need a sweater to stay warm, and so on. If my hair is falling out, I need to spend more time to look presentable, and then you need to factor in another five minutes for feeling badly that it took you two hours to do all this. I think she was starting to understand when she theoretically didn't even get to work, and she was left with six spoons. I then explained to her that she needed to choose the rest of her day wisely, since when your "spoons" are gone, they are gone. Sometimes you can borrow against tomorrow's "spoons", but just think how hard tomorrow will be with less "spoons". I also needed to explain that a person who is sick always lives with the looming thought that tomorrow may be the day that a cold comes, or an infection, or any number of things that could be very dangerous. So, you do not want to run low on "spoons", because you never know when you truly will need them. I didn't want to depress her, but I needed to be realistic, and unfortunately being prepared for the worst is part of a real day for me.

We went through the rest of the day, and she slowly learned that skipping lunch would cost her a spoon, as well as standing on a train, or even typing at her computer too long. She was forced to make choices and think about things differently. Hypothetically, she had to choose not to run errands, so that she could eat dinner that night. When we got to the end of her pretend day, she said she was hungry. I summarized that she had to eat dinner, but she only had one spoon left. If she cooked, she wouldn't have enough energy to clean the pots. If she went out for dinner, she might be too tired to drive home safely. Then, I also explained that I didn't even bother to add to this game, that she was so nauseous, that cooking was probably out of the question anyway. So, she decided to make soup, it was easy. I then said, 'It is only 7 pm, you have the rest of the night but maybe end up with one spoon, so you can do something fun, or clean your apartment, or do chores, but you can't do it all.'

I rarely see her emotional, so when I saw her upset, I knew maybe I was getting through to her. I didn't want my friend to be upset, but at the same time, I was happy to think finally maybe someone understood me a little bit. She had tears in her eyes and asked quietly, 'Christine, how do you do it? Do you really do this every day?' I explained that some days were worse than others; some days I have more spoons than most. But I can never make it go away and I can't forget about it, I always have to think about it. I handed her a spoon I had been holding in reserve. I said simply, 'I have learned to live life with an extra spoon in my pocket, in reserve. You need to always be prepared.'

It's hard, the hardest thing I ever had to learn is to slow down, and not do everything. I fight this to this day. I hate feeling left out, having to choose to stay home, or to not get things done that I want to. I wanted her to feel that frustration. I wanted her to understand, that everything everyone else does comes so easy, but for me, it is one hundred little jobs in one. I need to think about the weather, my temperature that day, and the whole day's plans before I can attack any one given thing. When other people can simply do things, I have to attack it and make a plan like I am strategizing a war. It is in that lifestyle, the difference between being sick and healthy. It is the beautiful ability to not think and just do. I miss that freedom. I miss never having to count "spoons". After we were emotional and talked about this for a little while longer, I sensed she was sad. Maybe, she finally understood. Maybe, she realized that she never could truly and honestly say she understands. But, at least now, she might not complain so much when I can't go out for dinner some nights, or when I never seem to make it to her house, and she always has to drive to mine. I gave her a hug when we walked out of the diner. I had the one spoon in my hand, and I said, 'Don't worry. I see this as a blessing. I have been forced to think about everything I do. Do you know how many spoons people waste every day? I don't have room for wasted time or wasted "spoons" and I chose to spend this time with you.'

Ever since that night, I have used the spoon theory to explain my life to many people. In fact, my family and friends refer to spoons all the time. It has been a code word for what I can and cannot do. Once people understand the spoon theory, they seem to understand me better, but I also think they live their life a little differently too. I think it isn't just good for understanding Lupus, but anyone dealing with any disability or illness. Hopefully, they don't take so much for granted or their life in general. I give a piece of myself, in every sense of the word when I do anything. It has become an inside joke. I have become famous for saying to people jokingly that they should feel special when I spend time with them, because they have one of my "spoons".

It is truly frightening to consider that you might only have another 30–35 years left to live. My mother passed away at sixty-two, and my father wanted to surpass his father's age (he passed away at seventy-one after a seven-year battle with throat, liver, and lung cancer); in my then crippled state, I couldn't see myself getting past seventy, and I would have been happy to get to sixty-five! I didn't want to succumb to my diagnosis; I wanted to fight and create a life worth living. With the knowledge I've gained over the years, my prognosis has remarkably improved, and finally, I can see beyond seventy—I even joked with a friend that my 100th birthday was going to be celebrated with top-shelf champagne and dancing on the table! I say this because I want you to know that there is a future for those who have been diagnosed with an autoimmune condition. It is possible to reverse your diagnosis, you can clear the hurdles, and you can live until you're 100! All it takes is commitment and motivation on your behalf to want a pain-free life with a full kit of spoons.

As a woman in her childbearing years, the question that people, surprisingly, were not afraid to ask was whether my autoimmune disease affected my ability to have children. Being a mother was a dream I'd had since I was little. I was always looking after friends' children and studied childcare when I finished school. But then I discovered how sick I had been when younger, and I just didn't know that I could go through the heartache of trying, conceiving, and possibly miscarrying; I told myself it would never happen (I also had a couple of not-very-nice partners who I could not see myself raising a child with). So, unfortunately, I cannot provide an answer because I never tried, and doctors won't be able to answer either until you begin trying; at least, that was their advice to me when I asked. Despite concerns about my fertility due to a poisoned uterus, doctors were not willing to run tests to determine whether it may be an issue for me.

My diagnosis, and lack of prognosis, launched me into self-preservation mode; I did everything I could to set myself up for the future in the event I could no longer work. I invested in property, a sound decision that I stick by to this day, but it meant I had two mortgages to facilitate, as neither property was positively geared; having a child would take me away from earning an income, and that would result in a default on my contract with the bank. I simply couldn't risk my financial security because I did not know how much longer I could continue employment at any level. Being a stubborn gal of Scottish descent, I also would not feel comfortable asking my partner to pay my debts while on maternity leave. Another consideration was, if this autoimmune disease were genetic, would I pass it on to my child? I couldn't risk that for them. Knowing what I know now, I would have been able to assist them in reversing their diagnosis, but I'm on the wrong side of forty to be contemplating bringing a life into this world.

When I was first diagnosed, I didn't know if I'd ever be able to get back to my 'normal' self—remember, my normal was not a normal, healthy person's normal; I was fatigued and weak from a young age. I would say I am now the healthiest, and fittest, I have ever been. Five years after diagnosis, when my health began to improve, I went hiking. Hiking! With a 10 kg backpack on my back! Now, that might seem trivial to most, but it was a huge achievement for me. There was a time, not long after my diagnosis, when I couldn't even walk around the block, let alone for 20.4 km carrying weight. There was no training involved (although, if this were a regular event, I'd probably put in a bit more effort); and, I booked out every Sunday to walk the local rail trails or hidden bush tracks with a friend, but without the heavy backpacks. To have made it down into Sealer's Cove through undulating terrain with that extra 10 kg was confirmation that I was on the right track with my health journey.

My way of living, this protocol, is about healing your entire body from the inside out to allow you to live a prosperous life. While at times it may be difficult, the process can be fun as you experiment with new food and take on new challenges and hobbies. You will develop an innate understanding of your body, what triggers your symptoms, what foods fuel your days, and what lifestyle changes provide the most benefit to you, just as you will learn what sacrifices and compromises you're willing to make for the sake of health.

By now you might be wondering what I did to reverse my diagnosis, which allowed me to live a pain-free life and get back to doing the things I love, which ultimately put me on this path of helping others. In the end, it was quite a simple solution, and yes, there are sceptics because it seems a little too simple, particularly as we have been brainwashed to trust doctors and not listen to our body's innate intelligence. Hippocrates said, 'All disease begins in the gut.' Therefore, all diseases should be healed through the gut, right? The principles I followed to overcome my autoimmune disease, are as follows:

- eat real, whole food
- live as low tox as possible
- make positive lifestyle changes
- develop your spirituality for deeper healing and nurturing.

My protocol is a combination of advice from many experts, although they all follow similar principles—eat whole, organic food; drink filtered water; bathe in the sunshine; embrace movement; practice mindfulness; and appreciate the time taken to rest. And it doesn't stop there. I will forever be reading and researching to ensure I, my clients, and readers are kept up to date with the latest in holistic health care and complementary therapies. While I no longer suffer from daily pain, I am aware that if I overindulge (and that could simply mean I've stayed up late to read a good book), I'm going to feel pretty crappy the next day. That's on me; I have an innate understanding of my body, and I make those decisions knowing exactly how they will affect me. Only you can change the path you're on. You can either decide to continue to live in pain, feeling like death warmed up every day, or you can choose to become an autoimmune warrior and get back to living!

I will go into more detail when I discuss what I have dubbed the Autoimmune Warrior Protocol, but first, we need to have a basic understanding of autoimmune diseases—what are they, how do they develop, how does the medical industry treat them, and finally, how do you cope when you receive a diagnosis?

Section 2:

Autoimmune Disease FAQs

If you don't take a little bit more time and money now for your health, you will have to take a lot more time and money later for illness.

—*Anonymous*

I believe, autoimmune diseases are on the rise. I believe, Mental health conditions are on the rise. Why? In my opinion, these health concerns have come about as our relationship with food has changed. Meals tend to be eaten on the go or off our laps in front of the TV. Families are busier these days with work commitments and children's sporting activities and extracurricular classes, so they miss out on time together to prepare and enjoy meals. Grocery stores and fast-food outlets have made it convenient to grab something quick and easy with little regard to ingredients and the manufacturing process. Our ancestors did not have the plethora of choices that we have today. They went out to hunt and forage for their food; everything was in its whole form—meat, vegetables, fruit, nuts, seeds—and they ate seasonally. They prepared meals from scratch and made their own sauces, condiments, and spreads.

Over the years, as technology and agricultural practices have developed, our bodies became accustomed to consuming processed food and chemicals; however, this does not mean we have evolved as a species to process these products, and consequently, the rate of illness and disease has increased.[2] Can you recall a time when you've used the excuses: 'Oh, I'm just getting older', or 'I must have overdone it on the footy field/cricket pitch/netball court', or 'I must not have had enough sleep last night; I'm really tired today'? We often disregard those niggly first symptoms, putting them down to overexertion and busy lifestyles. The initial go-to for someone experiencing symptoms such as a headache, stomach cramping, or joint pain is usually over-the-counter medication and supplements. It's not until they experience a 'can't get out of bed, feel paralysed' moment like I did that they begin to question what is occurring in their body.

Finding information and statistics on autoimmune diseases in Australia can be quite a mission. Search results include an overview of what constitutes an autoimmune disease, how they are diagnosed, and how they are treated; however, to find individual healthcare professionals offering a holistic solution to the many conditions that can

---

[2] C O'Meara, *Lab To Table*, Changing Habits, Australia, 2019.

be classified as autoimmune, one needs to have a mad set of investigative skills! If you search for 'reverse diagnosis of autoimmune condition', the top results are from Dr Amy Myers, Nutrition Consultant, and Mary Vance, Dr Will Cole, Dr Mark Hyman, and Dr Farrah, all in America, which can make attending information sessions challenging when they begin at 2 am Aussie time.

Yes, the population in America is greater than here in Australia, but with current figures estimating 5% of the Australian population are suffering from an autoimmune disease[3] (although I believe that figure would be much higher, as many remain undiagnosed), we are left at the mercy of our doctors, who admittedly 'don't know much' about these conditions. Surely, in a country of our size, we should have more accessibility to healthcare professionals who have studied these diseases as they would any other medical issue. This is why I have written this book for you and why I have qualified as an Autoimmune Paleo Certified Coach, trained by Dr Sarah Ballantyne (The Paleo Mom), Angie Alt, and Mickey Trescott, considered by many to be the godmothers of everything autoimmune.

What is an Autoimmune Disease?

In simple terms, an autoimmune disease develops when the immune system mistakenly attacks healthy cells,

---

[3] Statistic as stated by the Australasian Society Clinical Immunology and Allergy, 2022, https://allergy.org.au.

leading to inflammation and pain. Unfortunately, these diseases usually attack multiple organs or systems in the body—joints, skin, digestion, nerves, connective tissue, hormones, and muscles. There are over 100 currently recognised autoimmune conditions, and then there are those that have not yet been defined and don't seem to fit into the existing categories. Some of the more common autoimmune diseases are lupus, rheumatoid arthritis, fibromyalgia, chronic fatigue syndrome, multiple sclerosis, celiac disease, type 1 diabetes, Hashimoto's, and Lyme disease.[4]

I was not diagnosed on my first visit to the doctor. Several blood tests led to my diagnosis, and even then, it felt like they weren't 100% certain which category to put me in, as MCTD is an overlap disease, and also, I showed signs of Raynaud's phenomenon. My GP said it was rare and that there wasn't too much known about it, so I was referred to a rheumatologist.

In the beginning, I felt I could learn a lot from this specialist, his area of expertise was autoimmune conditions, he knew how these diseases brought about pain, swelling, and stiffness in the body, and he should be able to advise on the best solution to fix it. Of course, I was working on the assumption that the specialist would operate like a chiropractor; fix the immediate problem then focus on maintenance.

---

[4] S Ballantyne, *The Paleo Approach*, Victory Belt Publishing, Canada, 2013.

I compiled a list of questions, eager to pick his brain: 'What is the prognosis for someone with MCTD?', 'Is there a cure?', 'How will this disease affect my organs?', 'Are there tests to measure the size of my organs now and in the future to determine if my condition is worsening?', 'How much longer can I expect to be working?', 'Is this genetic, and can I pass it on to a baby?', 'What are the natural therapies that I can utilise to reduce the symptoms?'

My first appointment was about 15–20 minutes, and every appointment after that, ten minutes. My questions went unanswered; his solution was to undergo regular blood and lung function tests and to take medication … for the rest of my life. I admit that response did not float my boat, but I was in so much pain that I got the script for hydroxychloroquine filled. Yes, the same hydroxychloroquine that the government banned new prescriptions of in 2020, at the height of the pandemic, and the drug that I discovered an allergy to—obviously my body's way of telling me that drugs are not the answer. When he prescribed methotrexate, which for those in the know is a drug used in cancer treatment, I decided I'd had enough of that particular merry-go-round and I got off the horse.

What Factors Contribute to Autoimmune Disease?

Name a symptom, I've had it—dry mouth, flaky skin, chest pain, fatigue, frozen fingers, and toes, muscle weakness, shortness of breath, hair loss, stomach cramps, joint aches and pains, swollen glands, nausea, reflux, diarrhea, brain fog, sleep disturbances. These can all be very debilitating to living a normal life, especially if it's a day that requires close contact with the toilet! So, what caused these symptoms to develop? What I learned was there are four factors that play a role in the development of an autoimmune disease:

- genetics
- environment
- trauma
- diet and lifestyle (exercise, sleep, stress).

Genetics

Let's start with genetics. Was there a family history of autoimmune-related conditions in my family? Mum had passed away two years before my diagnosis, so I couldn't ask her, and Dad, well, we know by now that Dad ignored my plight at first, stating that he didn't think there was anything wrong with me because I 'looked well' and could withstand some form of chiropractic adjustment (any autoimmune sufferer will tell you there are times when something as innocuous as a chiropractic adjustment can feel like every bone in your body is breaking and even the lightest touch can cause immense pain). But no, there was no family history on Dad's side.

I would later find out that we did have medical issues on both sides—breast, throat, lung, and liver cancer (that's a lot of cancer, should I be concerned?), heart disease, myocardial fibrosis, renal impairment—but how did that relate to me now, and did it matter when I'm my own person with the ability to change the trajectory of my health journey? Just because my family was afflicted with these conditions didn't mean I had to be, and with this knowledge, I could change my outcome; I did not have to succumb to my genetics any more than I had to succumb to the medical industry.

Environment

Moving on to the environment. What chemicals had I been exposed to? Was there something in my environment that could have triggered this widespread inflammation? I grew up near coal-fired power stations, but other than that, I wouldn't have said my environment was all that toxic. Okay, Mum didn't mind a bit of Roundup in the yard and used chemically based cleaning products, but could that cause an autoimmune reaction? *Yes*! I believe these products certainly contributed to my weakened state.

I recently read Stephanie Seneff's book, *Toxic Legacy*, about how glyphosate, the active ingredient in Roundup, is destroying our health and that of the environment. I used brightly coloured flags to highlight points that were relevant to autoimmune disease, only to realise that was pretty much the entire book! Seneff confirms that glyphosate is inflammatory to the microbiome and this disruption can cause immune dysregulation and autoimmune disease.[5]

---

[5] S Seneff, *Toxic Legacy*, Chelsea Green Publishing, United Kingdom, 2021, p 153.

Now, you might think that your exposure to glyphosate is minute and not worth concern, but something toxic, given in smaller quantities, does not make it any less toxic, and unfortunately, glyphosate is a chemical that likes to hang around in the soil, in waterways, in the air, and in our bodies. Whatever we can do now to lessen the load on our bodies and the environment will pay off in the long term.

Trauma

Let's consider trauma. This could be psychological or physical. For me, it was a big tick in this box. I mentioned peritonitis earlier; for those that don't know what that is, it is inflammation of the peritoneum, the membrane that lines the inner abdominal wall and encloses organs within the abdomen. In my case, the peritonitis was brought on by the ruptured appendix. I spent a couple of weeks in hospital, Mum sleeping on a trundle bed beside me, and upon reflection, that was the beginning of my journey; my body was never quite right after that. By the time I was released from hospital for the second time, my poor body was traumatised. I had been cut open and filled with a plethora of drugs—I'd never even taken paracetamol before; imagine how hard my body had to work to process those drugs on top of what it was already fighting.

Diet and Exercise

Finally, diet and lifestyle. I held onto the belief that I ate well when growing up, yet on reflection, my diet consisted of a variety of bread, cereals, and other grains (I loved nothing more than having a bowl of Crunchy Nut® cornflakes with cream after dinner) with a small amount of protein and vegetables. Oh, but then I went through a vegetarian stage as a teenager, eliminating the small amount of protein that I was consuming. So, in hindsight, my diet wasn't that great, despite Mum's fantastic home-cooked meals (she was bloody good at Italian food, and to this day, I blame that for my love of pasta).

Of course, we must also consider my role model when it came to eating habits.

I cannot recall Mum sitting down to enjoy a meal with us when I was young; certainly, when I was older, we enjoyed many meals together after my parents separated, but when I was a child, I just remember her working hurriedly in the kitchen.

I remember her saying years later that it was difficult catering to three different meal preferences (my brother ate nothing but chicken schnitzel or nuggets, I was vegetarian, and Dad would eat whatever he was given) and that had resulted in a lack of enthusiasm to eat. She would also graze as she cooked, which I find myself doing too. A raw vegetable here and there as you prepare, a spoonful of sauce or several as you get the seasoning just right, a bit of bread with butter to quell the hunger, but it's slightly too much and ruins your appetite. There was also some reliance on the information provided, in that a Healthy Diet Pyramid was released and became gospel.

Cereals were healthy because they came from corn or wheat. Bread was healthy, but better if it was multigrain. Pasta constituted a fantastic meal, as it provided energy; athletes would carb-load before a game or event, which must mean pasta is beneficial for endurance. Meat provided a good dose of protein and should be eaten regularly for muscle development; there was nothing sinister about a nice cut of steak!

Okay, so it's common sense that if we don't sleep well or move as much as we should or let the stressors of everyday life get to us, then our health will suffer. And if this continues for months, even years, then it begins to affect how we approach daily life. While it's easy to say this is common sense, sometimes life just gets so busy that we forget to take care of ourselves, allowing stress and negativity to flow into our energy.

Like most parents, Mum would tell me stories of when I was born and how I behaved as an infant, and one of the things that I remember her telling me was that I never slept well as a baby. I asked her to clarify this; did I cry, chuck a tantrum, go looking for a party …? 'No, you didn't cry,' she said. 'You just laid there, looking at the ceiling, as though you were contemplating how to make your mark on the world.' I'm not sure that my sleeping habits got any better as I got older; I always felt tired, I always had dark circles under my eyes, and I always felt foggy. Of course, the lack of sleep meant I didn't focus too well when at school and would often find my thoughts drifting to anything other than what was being presented (again, could be the Pisces in me!).

I'm not quite sure how I managed it at the time, but when I reached the senior campus of secondary school, I decided I would walk to and from school every day. That was an 8 km round trip! And I didn't always eat lunch, so where did I find that energy? Intuitively, I think my body was telling me I needed to keep moving. You wouldn't necessarily think being a kid is that stressful, but think about how you might feel when a teacher tells you that you have to decide what you want to do for the rest of your life when you're fifteen years old, or the pressure that you may feel from parents and teachers during your last couple of years at school to achieve that near-perfect ENTER score (now known as an ATAR, or Australian Tertiary Admission Rank), or when you experience bullying or when your parents argue so often that they eventually decide to separate.

Kids take on a lot more burden than we realise, and all that stress contributes to an unhealthy disposition. FYI, the last two factors played a huge role in my not receiving a great uni score. It was slightly above average, and there was no way, at fifteen years of age, I could definitively state what I wanted to do for the rest of my working days; in fact, most adults have about eight careers before settling on one that they enjoy. What a stressful time for a teenager, especially one as empathetic as me, who often felt during those years that the weight of the world was upon my shoulders.

These four factors provided the perfect storm for my autoimmune disease to develop. Maybe it would have been easier to list what doesn't cause an autoimmune disease, because the four items that I have listed are everything that life consists of; by this reasoning, everyone should have an autoimmune disease! In my opinion, they probably do. But now is not the time to become disheartened; now is the time to feel empowered because all these things can be changed for you to live a healthier, robust life. With this knowledge, and with your own research, you can target the factors that will make the most difference to your overall health and those that will ultimately kick your autoimmune condition to the curb. You, too, can heal and strengthen your body—this is an exciting proposition!

What Is Leaky Gut and What Roles Does it Play in Autoimmune Disease?

The human gut is home to trillions of bacteria, some good and some, not so good. This rich diversity of bacteria is vital to health, as it promotes nutrient absorption and strengthens the immune system. Without these bacteria, or when the seemingly good bacteria become pathogenic, we are left vulnerable to developing digestive disorders, skin issues, food allergies, candida, and autoimmune diseases due to reduced immunity.

Leaky gut, the simple term for intestinal permeability, occurs when undigested proteins, lectins, or environmental toxins pass through the intercellular tight junctions of the gut lining into the bloodstream, promoting local and systemic immune responses that we recognise as inflammation.[6]

Food is not the only factor to influence a leaky gut; stress, sleep deprivation, chemicals inhaled or absorbed, medications, and negativity all play their part as well.[7] With that in mind, it is not surprising that leaky gut has shown up in tests conducted on those with autoimmune diseases, including rheumatoid arthritis, celiac disease, Crohn's disease, diabetes, and multiple sclerosis.[8] Given that diet is a common denominator in both, as with the age-old chicken or egg dilemma, one could question which comes first—the autoimmune disease or leaky gut? Either way, we are susceptible to some intense, damaging immune responses.

How Are Autoimmune Diseases Treated?

A general practitioner will prescribe medication, including NSAIDs (anti-inflammatories), corticosteroids (suppresses inflammation), antibiotics, disease-modifying antirheumatic drugs—DMARDs (suppresses the immune system, calm the autoimmune process), and biologic DMARDs (mimics the biological activity in the body).

---

[6] A Lerner, Changes in intestinal tight junction permeability associated with industrial food additives explain the rising incidence of autoimmune disease, Autoimmunity Reviews, 2015, pp 479-489.
[7] A Alt, *The Autoimmune Wellness Handbook,* Rodale, New York, 2016.
[8] S Ballantyne, *The Paleo Approach,* Victory Belt Publishing, Canada, 2013.

As I've mentioned, I was initially prescribed medication. If I had not been allergic to hydroxychloroquine, would I still be on it today? No, I don't believe so. My background was very much focused on natural healing, so I would have found my way back to healing without medication in time.

I am not suggesting that you give up your medication. What I am encouraging you to do is to listen to your body, keep a journal, and speak to your doctor about reducing the dosage over time; you might find that by making changes to diet and lifestyle and undertaking holistic therapies, you are able to wean off the medication. I also offer this advice: if you have a doctor who is not willing to discuss how natural therapies can benefit you or work collaboratively with your healthcare team, find a new doctor. When managing an autoimmune disease, it must be looked at from a holistic perspective; that is, everything about you, your body, your diet, and your lifestyle must be considered because all these factors work together.

You may also consider natural treatment, which is commonly known as an alternative or complementary approach. What is 'alternative' about treating our bodies in an organic, natural way? By their own admission, my doctors told me they had no idea what MCTD was all about, yet they expected me to trust that they knew how to manage my condition. I was not comfortable taking medication, given that I'd never so much as looked at a packet of paracetamol over the years. There are many modalities out there—chiropractic, massage, Reiki, kinesiology, physiotherapy, floating, acupuncture. Once you've spent a bit of time looking into your diagnosed condition, you will learn that there are many others out there who have faced similar battles, and similar hurdles, and are now sharing their knowledge. It's not a one-size-fits-all approach, but it's a starting point.

Coping with a Diagnosis

You've won a share in the ill health lottery—now what? Receiving a diagnosis does not simplify anything for someone suffering from an autoimmune disease; in fact, it often makes the situation ten times worse as you deal with mixed emotions and the jumble of thoughts and questions going through your head.

Initially, you may be relieved that you've got that diagnosis and start formulating your plan of attack, until you realise the doctors are no better at sourcing information than the average Joe on the street. You may grieve, particularly as the doctors don't provide much hope when they reveal what you are up against, and you can lose all those bright visions of how your life was going to pan out. You might even feel as though you are alone in your battle as your family and friends fail to understand what is happening. After all, you can barely comprehend it yourself, so it must seem impossible to ask for their support. And then you may become anxious about the impending changes: to what extent will you be physically disabled, how much will you have to rely on others, how often might you be hospitalised, how will your illness affect your or your family's finances, will you be able to maintain employment and for how long ... For you to be able to withstand the onslaught of emotions after diagnosis, you need to learn resilience. Your diagnosis is not a life sentence, although it may feel like that at the time, and you do not have to let it define who you are and how you live. You can practice resilience in a few ways, so let's go over some.

Not freaking out—handling the situation in a calm, composed manner. If you feel anxious, spend a moment taking a few deep breaths and work on adjusting your mindset.

Taking charge of the things you can control. We spend so much time lamenting things that are out of our control. What a waste of energy! Why not focus on what we can control and actively seek solutions to the problem, as you did when you picked up this book? You are a survivor, not a victim; be resourceful, research your condition, look for others who have also experienced your symptoms/illness/feelings, etc.

Remaining positive and believing in yourself. You have more strength and confidence than you realise. Look for positive aspects in each situation and as you go about the day.

Establish healthy coping strategies—laugh, get some exercise, meditate, ditch the literary fiction and read a light, laugh-out-loud novel (Marian Keyes or Kathy Lette are my go-to authors), enjoy a leisurely lunch with friends, or spend quality time with your family.

Section 3:

The Autoimmune Warrior Protocol

I did then what I knew to do. Now that I know better, I do better.

—Maya Angelou

There is no-one more qualified to talk about autoimmune disease than someone who has lived, or is living, with a chronic illness. The information in this section relates to the steps I took to heal my body, but this may not be the case for everyone. I have taken snippets of advice from many professionals and read, and continue to read, many, many books to determine what works for me.

This protocol is not designed to heal you overnight; your body has spent considerable time working itself into a state of inflammation, so you will need to show yourself some love and respect and provide time and space for healing.

Your recovery will depend on several factors, including how committed you are to getting better, how leaky your gut may be, what antibodies your body is producing, the damage done to cells, tissues, and organs, and how dysregulated your hormones have become, but, most importantly, how positive your mindset is. Remember, I've spent the better part of ten years in this cycle, at times noncommittal, so you will only get out what you put in.

I have seen many posts from friends on Facebook talking about a certain autoimmune condition as it affects them or a family member. As you might have noticed, I'm fairly open about my health issues and what I have been able to accomplish, so they're fully aware of my history when I mention that I can assist them to overcome their condition. I mean, no-one wants to live with daily pain, right? Imagine my surprise when the feedback to me has been, 'Oh, it's not that bad at the moment', or 'I'm not experiencing a flare right now; I just wanted to share the information'. *What?!* Despite being diagnosed with an autoimmune disease and experiencing daily, debilitating symptoms, my friends, for whatever reason, believe it's not possible to feel or live better. They have become their diagnosis; they believe that this is the hand they've been dealt and there's no way out other than to take the medication the doctor prescribes. You only get one body, so why would you not provide it with premium fuel so it functions optimally?

One of the first tasks I undertook was to collect all my test results. Blood, urine, lung function, whatever the doctor or specialist had on file, I asked for copies. I became quite adept at interpreting the results; the fact that the areas of concern are written in bold numbering certainly helped, but

I took it one step further and researched all the acronyms associated with the test. CRP, C-reactive protein, measures the level of inflammation in the blood. ESR, erythrocyte sedimentation rate, is another marker for inflammation in the blood. ANA, antinuclear antibody—the presence of these in the blood indicates an autoimmune disease may be present. WCC, white blood cell count, obviously measures the number of white blood cells in the blood; these cells fight infection and inflammation, so if they're low, you're in trouble. And I continued to research all these and more until I had notes on everything and what could affect those counts, both in the positive and negative.

The second was to look at my diet. What we eat and how we eat determines how we function; without the right food, we lack energy and fall flat throughout the day. Eating processed food is not designed to fuel us for any length of time (how many times have you eaten fast food, such as McDonald's, and felt hungry an hour later?), but was there specific food that I needed to focus on to alleviate my symptoms, and what food did I need to avoid, other than the obvious? What role does slowing down and chewing food properly play in digestion and reduction of symptoms? Is there really any evidence as to why you shouldn't eat just before bed; I mean, don't we all have a big Christmas lunch and fall asleep afterward? What's the issue? Apparently there are many issues with scoffing food and sleeping shortly thereafter, the main one being that you're interfering with the proper digestion of food and that may present in some embarrassing symptoms (gas) and some that are uncomfortable (bloating, reflux).

The third was to look at my environment and lifestyle. What was I exposed to in my everyday life that could affect my autoimmune condition? As it turns out, quite a lot! I began to take note of everything that I used on my skin, in the kitchen, in the laundry, everything that was in my office, external to the office, around my home, even the items that seem trivial that could have a huge impact on my health.

Once the basics were implemented and my health was regained, it was time to look further afield—spirituality and its role in health and wellbeing.

Nutrition

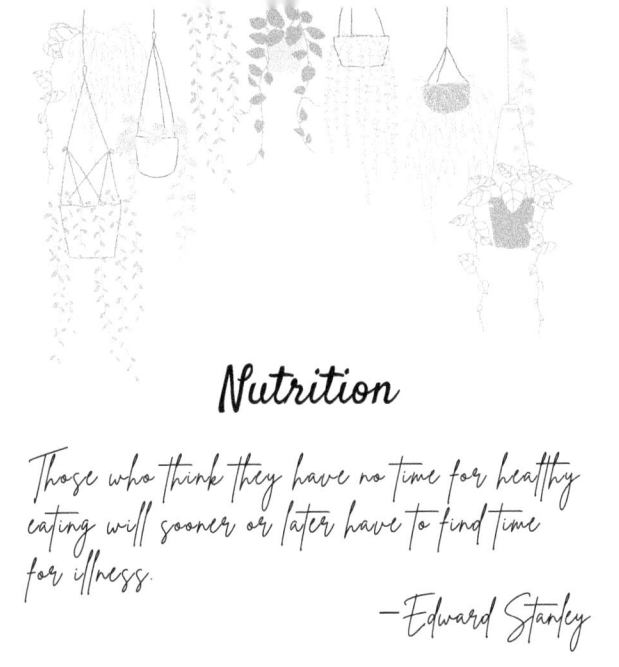

Those who think they have no time for healthy eating will sooner or later have to find time for illness.

—Edward Stanley

I believe the Standard Australian Diet is woeful (you only have to look at the acronym to realise this). When eating healthy, real, whole food is considered a 'diet', it feels as though we've almost lost the battle against the manufacturers. I feel I was somewhat lucky in that I had a stay-at-home mum (which is rather rare these days, as mums often return to the workforce to help support their families) who believed in eating whole foods and cooking nutritious meals for her family. While this way of eating was instilled in me in my formative years, I didn't always stick to it as I got older. Did that exacerbate my autoimmune condition? You bet! I moved out of home when I was nineteen and battled for a few years to keep my head above water, which meant a tight budget and cheap food options, lots of pasta and rice. This way of eating was not conducive to good health, as I would find out. The way I eat now is a return to the days of old—real, whole food with no additives, preservatives, numbers, or colours. Out of curiosity, have a look at the ingredients label on the food items in your fridge and pantry—can you pronounce the ingredients? Do you know what the ingredients are? Are there additives and preservatives? Is any ingredient followed by a number? Why does your product not just contain whole foods? Ingredients found in nature! I believe the human body is an organic being, that it requires organic nutrients to function and develop properly, and I question how a 'food' item processed and manufactured in a factory, full of chemical additives, is beneficial to the body's way of functioning.

'It's Convenient'

Don't eat anything your great-great-grandmother wouldn't recognise as food. There are a great many foodlike items in the supermarket your ancestors wouldn't recognise as food ... stay away from these.

—Michael Pollan, 'Unhappy Meals', New York Times, January 28 2007.

The phrase I receive most from people is 'it's convenient', followed closely by 'I don't have time'. Sound familiar? Well, it may be convenient now to grab that pastry or frozen meal, but it won't be convenient in the coming years when your body begins to fail and you have more health problems than you can count. Will you have the time then to focus on your health? Murphy's Law dictates that the moment your health crisis becomes a serious issue, you will be busier than ever, looking after children, attempting to hold down a job, caring for elderly parents, and so on. Yes, that may sound harsh, but it's fact. I should know; I've lived through it. And maybe you are too, but you've convinced yourself that it's just because you're getting older or because you had a late night and didn't get adequate sleep ... The best advice I can give to fellow sufferers who claim these foods are convenient is prep, prep, prep! Once I was well enough, I would spend a weekend in the kitchen (yes, I was exhausted after a week of work and would have preferred to be sitting in my library, reading a novel, but that would not be conducive to health), preparing and cooking several different meals, portioning and freezing. I had lunches and dinners for at least a month, and that meant I could not possibly be tempted by the lip-smacking, carb-loaded spaghetti Bolognese pizza that I used to enjoy on a regular basis (note: 'regular' should be interpreted as every week; I was an absolute mess, and the smell of the sauce and melted cheese was my kryptonite).

At the very least, if you don't have the energy to create full meals, cut up your vegetables and meat and store them in the fridge for later use. This is a great option if you have a slow cooker (no, they are not just winter appliances for stews and casseroles), as you can throw everything in the pot in the morning and by the time you return home for the day, your dinner is ready and the house will smell divine.

Elimination or Substitution

The food you eat can either be the safest and most powerful form of medicine or the slowest form of poison.

— Ann Wigmore

I've come to learn that education about food and nutrition can be rather controversial. I've lost count of the number of times people look at me, mouth agape, at the suggestion that they eat granola or a chia pudding for breakfast as opposed to their usual cereal or toast with margarine and sugary jam, or, dare I say it, their beloved Vegemite.

Often it is not about needing to eliminate a food group but substituting one food for another, making smarter choices for the benefit of your health. However, when it comes to additives, preservatives, colours, flavours, and numbers, I believe there is no room for compromise—they should all be eliminated. These are chemical compounds that will build in the body over time, weakening the gut lining and immune system, leading to inflammation and pain.[9] Not an ideal place for an autoimmune sufferer to be.

---

[9] A Lerner, Changes in intestinal tight junction permeability associated

Substitutions

I've specifically noted the following two groups of substitutions, as these are the controversial foods that I have the most arguments over. Yes, there are still people that believe margarine and vegetable oils are good for you because they are marketed as such, and for these people, ignorance is bliss—what you don't know, you can't action.

Margarine vs butter—when people say cheap and nasty, I'm sure they're talking about margarine. Margarine was developed in the mid-19th century when Europe experienced a recession in farming and communities demanded a cheap, shelf-stable substitute.[10] A French chemist by the name of Hippolyte Mege Mouries invented and patented the spread using animal fats and artificial gastric juice. These days, margarine is made with a blend of vegetable oils, emulsifiers, preservatives, food acids, flavourings, and colourings.[11] I do not consider this to be a healthy food product, nor do I use products marketed as 'spreadable' (think olive oil spread). I advocate for food in its whole form and choose butter or ghee over margarine. These are products that contain cow milk fat or cream, and that's it, no preservatives, additives, or any other nasties that irritate the microbiome.

---

with industrial food additives explain the rising incidence of autoimmune disease, Autoimmunity Reviews, 2015.
[10] A Williams, *Margarine*, Pergamon Press Ltd., London, 1954, p. 2
[11] Flora fact sheet, https://www.floraspread.com.au

Vegetable oil vs olive oil—vegetable oil sounds healthy, but it's up there with margarine as one of the worst foods to consume due to it being a partially hydrogenated oil containing trans fats, which have been shown to cause inflammation and calcification of arterial cells.[12] Additionally, any other hydrogenated, or partially hydrogenated, oil (safflower, cottonseed, rapeseed, canola, soybean) should be avoided at all costs. These oils are manufactured to preserve shelf life and contain trans fats that can raise cholesterol and result in other health complications, for example, cancer.[13]

Below are common substitutions so you can still enjoy your favourite meals, just using different ingredients:

Rice ☛ cauliflower rice
Spaghetti ☛ zoodles (zucchini noodles)
Potato ☛ sweet potato or pumpkin
Milk chocolate ☛ dark chocolate
Margarine ☛ butter or ghee (for those who are lactose intolerant)
Vegetable oil ☛ olive oil
Soft drink ☛ kombucha
Wheat flour ☛ almond meal/coconut meal/tapioca flour.

---

[12] F Kummerow, The negative effects of hydrogenated trans fats and what to do about them, Atherosclerosis, 2009, pp 458-465.
[13] I Laake, Intake of trans fatty acids from partially hydrogenated vegetable and fish oils and ruminant fat in relation to cancer risk, International Journal of Cancer, 2012, pp 1389-1403.

The Paleo/Keto Approach

The doctor of the future will no longer treat the human frame with drugs, but rather will cure and prevent disease with nutrition.
— Thomas Edison

The paleo/keto approach focuses on consuming a diet high in protein (red meat, poultry, seafood, eggs, offal), vegetables, and fats and oils (avocado, coconut oil, tallow, olives, etc) as opposed to cereals and grains. Berries are the preferred fruit to eat due to their low levels of fructose, and oily nuts and seeds rate highly among the other foods to enjoy on this diet. Generally, it is recommended that carbohydrate intake is between 100–200 g per day if the sources of your carbs are whole fruit and vegetables.[14] The concern among people when first confronted with the thought of eliminating bread, cereals, and grains is what will be left to eat. As you'll learn, there is plenty, and you'll find that you

---

[14] S Ballantyne, *Paleo Principles*, Victory Belt Publishing, Canada, 2017.

won't feel like you need to reach for the snacks as often as you would eating the standard diet because you'll be satiated. We need to move away from the programming that we endured as children, the thought that what is marketed at us (notice I said 'at', not 'to') is best for our health, that the manufacturers know what our bodies need. Our bodies crave real, organic food; that is its premium fuel, and that's what we need to be feeding ourselves and our families.

Note: nightshade vegetables can prove to be problematic for autoimmune sufferers. More detail on this in the next chapter.

Trigger foods

Every human being is the author of his own health or disease.

— Buddha

There are a few inflammatory foods for autoimmune sufferers, and I will go through them below. Now, this might not be the case for everyone, so I would follow an elimination then reintroduction process to determine specifically which foods inflame your gut. The Autoimmune Paleo Approach, developed by Sarah Ballantyne, is a thorough elimination/reintroduction protocol for those wanting to go all in, and it is the foundation from which I developed my protocol.

Gluten-containing Foods

I once went to a naturopath who, on first inspection of my blood under a microscope, stated, 'Wow, you're really messed up!' Yep, that's why I made the appointment; now tell me how I can heal! Of course, the first step was to eliminate gluten. At the time, I didn't understand why gluten was such an issue, and I didn't research it properly until I began studying in 2019. *What's wrong with bread?* The way we grow and process wheat has contributed to our sensitivity to gluten. Our ancestors used to mill and ferment wheat in such a way that our bodies could digest it.

Nowadays, the crops are sprayed with chemicals, the product is processed in a factory, more chemicals are added to increase taste (think along the lines of sugar and associated substitutes) and shelf life, and the list goes on ... We are already dealing with environmental toxic overload and stress, so ingesting more toxins seems to me like a recipe for ill health.

Gluten is one of the worst offenders for anyone dealing with an autoimmune disease and even those who aren't. I've had people say that it doesn't give them any problems, to which I respond, 'For now ...' followed by an explanation. Now, I don't want to bog you down with a biology lesson, so, in layman's terms, the consumption of gluten, which most people consume on daily basis, results in little tears being formed in the lining of your gut. When you're young, these little tears will heal themselves, but as you age, the little tears stop healing and the gap in the gut lining means those toxins that you consume now have the ability to enter your bloodstream as undigested particles, wreaking havoc. Your blood cells will become stuck together and oxygen will struggle to get through, causing discomfort in the form of gas, bloating, stomach cramps, and diarrhea.[15] And to think most of us were brought up being advised to eat 'twelve

---

[15] S Ballantyne, *The Paleo Approach*, Victory Belt Publishing, Canada, 2013.

serves of breads and cereals each day'! I remember saying to mum when I was in my teens, 'If I ate twelve serves of bread and cereals, I'd be the size of a house!' Innately, I knew that food was not serving my body. So, I eliminated gluten. Sounds simple, but this step requires a discerning eye. Many products contain gluten, so ensure you read the ingredient labels thoroughly and have a basic understanding of the other ingredients that manufacturers add to food that may contain gluten. In addition, remove all foods labelled 'gluten-free' from the diet. While these foods may not contain gluten, the gluten component must be replaced by something, and it is often a synthetic compound that allows the other ingredients to bind together, replicating the effect gluten would have if it were an ingredient in the food.

Sugar

Consumption of sugar has increased dramatically over the past several decades, sometimes unknowingly, as sugar is added to almost every food that sits on a supermarket shelf. Unfortunately, the consumption of foods high in refined sugar encourages the growth of bad bacteria in the gut, diminishing intestinal permeability and provoking the immune system to instigate inflammation. Not only does sugar inflame the gut microbiome, but it can also have the potential to cause cognitive dysfunction via the brain-gut connection. Studies have shown a diet high in sugar could compromise blood-brain barrier integrity, promote neuroinflammation, reduce short-chain fatty acid production (essential for cognitive function), and promote endotoxemia, which has been linked to memory impairment.[16] I believe much of the Australian population develops a sugar addiction from early childhood. Not surprising when you consider that since the Healthy Eating Pyramid was introduced in 1982, we've been loading our bowls with an entire day's sugar intake for breakfast! A typical breakfast for a child in the 80s was cereal or toast/crumpets with some sort of spread, vegemite, peanut butter, or jam. Some kids might have even had fruit yogurt and washed it all down with juice or maybe a flavoured milk. Look at the sugar content on a cereal box and the milk carton. For food that is supposed to come from grains, why does it contain so much sugar? Is the sugar in milk naturally produced, or is that something manufacturers have added during the pasteurisation or homogenisation process? Consider the label on the bread bag. Why does bread need to contain sugar? Then have a look at the sugar that goes into your spread. Oh, and don't forget about the yogurt and juice, especially if it's labelled more as a fruit drink and doesn't contain 100% natural fruit juice. And that's just the beginning of the day! Not much has changed as the years have gone by; food manufacturers feed off of people's addiction to sugar.

The other week, I watched my partner's daughter get her breakfast: an Up 'N' Go drink, coffee-flavoured

---

[16] E Noble, Gut to Brain Dysbiosis: Mechanisms Linking Western Diet Consumption, the Microbiome and Cognitive Impairment, Frontiers in Behavioural Science, 2017.

sachet, instant oat porridge with honey, and a muesli bar. I calculated 22 grams of sugar just in what she ate and drank for breakfast! I was horrified.

Now, not all sugar is bad; it's the refined white stuff you don't want to include in your daily food consumption. I don't use sugar a lot, but when I do, I choose rapadura or coconut sugar. Alternatively, you could use a natural sweetener, such as honey or maple syrup. As Mum used to say, everything in moderation. While you may tolerate the healthier sweeteners, to ascertain which foods incite inflammation, sugar in all forms should be eliminated. You might even find that when the time comes to reintroduce sugar, your sensitivity to the sweet stuff may have altered and you might not want to include it in your diet. I always had a strong sweet tooth as a kid, but now I much prefer to sit down to a cheese platter than a cake or slice. Additionally, artificial sweeteners should also be avoided.

A few years ago, even before I was diagnosed with my autoimmune disease, my friend, not yet forty, told me that she had been experiencing pain, weight gain, headaches, dizziness, and fatigue. She was in such a bad state that she was using a cane to assist her with walking. She had been to several doctors and specialists and tested for everything from chronic fatigue to arthritis to cancer, yet no-one had any answers for her. That is until one of these specialists asked her what her diet consisted of and she revealed that she drank a few cans of diet coke every day. Now they were getting somewhere. The manufacturers of diet and zero-sugar drinks remove the refined sugar and add a synthetic chemical named aspartame, which is a neurotoxin and nerve irritator. I'm sure the intelligent reader can guess what some of the side effects include and what diseases it can induce. Dizziness, headaches, weight gain, seizures, depression, Alzheimer's, lupus, multiple sclerosis, cancer, and liver disease.[17] Sound familiar? My friend had all these symptoms and was tested for all those health complaints. Naturally, the doctor asked her to eliminate these drinks to see if the symptoms cleared up. Within a few weeks, her symptoms had improved. Keep in mind that this toxicity had built up over many years, so it took some time for her body to heal, but she did heal.

Dairy

Many people have discovered they are lactose intolerant, which might seem odd, as we were all brought up on milk, right? I'd estimate that 98% of people transitioned from breast or formula feeding straight onto cow's milk. Some may have taken an extra step and started with goat's milk before cow's milk; it has been suggested that this is because goat's milk is comparable to breast milk and makes for an easier transition to cow's milk.[18] But I ask you this: do we

---

[17] P Humphries, *Direct and indirect cellular effects of aspartame on the brain*, European Journal of Clinical Nutrition, 2008, pp 451-462.

[18] Y Liu, Functional comparison of breast milk, cow milk and goat milk based on changes in the intestinal flora of mice, LWT, 2021.

even need milk? Most people will respond, 'Of course, we do; milk provides calcium to prevent osteoporosis!' In fact, there are many other foods that we can derive calcium from, such as dark, leafy green vegetables, sardines, nuts, and seeds. Unfortunately, the pasteurisation and homogenisation process strips milk of essential enzymes required for humans to properly digest the product, hence why many discover an intolerance to lactose (sugar) or casein (protein). Milk also contains protease inhibitors, which contribute to the development of a leaky gut; it is insulinogenic, which contributes to insulin resistance and inflammation; and it contains bovine hormones that can alter our hormone levels. Phew, that's quite a lot to be aware of!

If cheese is your main food group (as I often treat it), the process to eliminate can be quite difficult. Milk, however, I had no problems cutting out, which was interesting given that I would drink it by the gallon when I was coming down with a cold. Yes, a cold, when dairy should be the last thing craved, but for my brother and I, it was our go-to. These days, I don't drink it by the glass, let alone the gallon, and if there is a recipe requiring milk, I substitute coconut or almond milk. I will, however, occasionally get a takeaway coffee with full-fat milk, which doesn't disturb my gut, but I wouldn't want to have one every day—trust me when I say it's not fun searching for a loo when your gut is cramping and you're trying really hard to keep your cheeks clenched!

Soy

The main food choice for those who are vegetarian or lactose intolerant. I believe this stems from the perception that it is consumed in large quantities in Asian countries; therefore, it must be okay. Having been to Japan and Vietnam, I know that soy is not the main ingredient in their dishes; it is used sparingly. However, soy has exploded in the Western market, becoming a major ingredient in many foods, and many of this is hidden—cake and bread mixes, cookies, crackers, spreads, sauces, and even infant formula. Unfortunately, soy, and soy-related ingredients can cause immense gastrointestinal distress. Foods to be mindful of include:

- bean curd
- edamame
- hydrolysed soy protein
- miso
- monosodium glutamate (MSG)
- soy lecithin (also marketed as soy protein/isolate)
- soybean (curds, granules)
- tamari
- teriyaki sauce
- textured vegetable protein (TVP)
- tofu.

Corn

Who doesn't love a warm corn cob with melted butter?! When I was young, returning home from school, I used to get a can of corn from the cupboard, pour it into a bowl, chuck it in the microwave for a minute, then slather half a tub of butter over those juicy little kernels. Delicious! Little did I know, the only healthy component of that dish was the butter—both the corn and the microwave that I heated it in were hazardous to my health. Like soy, the corn produced these days is most likely a GMO—genetically modified organism. GMO seeds are engineered specifically to contain compounds to protect the seed, making them resistant to insecticide and pesticide sprays. The list of corn-containing ingredients is long. Have a google of what corn is used in—I think you'll be quite shocked! I will include a few of them here, but if I were you, I'd still be doing an ingredient check, especially if the product contains additives or preservatives (not that you should be consuming these anyway, but you might be interested in what your pantry has to offer):

Artificial flavourings	Artificial sweeteners	Ascorbic acid	Aspartame
Baking powder	Barley malt	Brown sugar	Calcium citrate
Calcium lactate	Caramel and caramel colour	Cellulose	Citric acid
Dextrose	Ethanol	Fructose	Glucose
Lecithin	Maize	Maltodextrin	Polysorbate
Xanthan gum	Xylitol	Yeast	

Okay, so I may have listed more than I said I would, but they are all common corn-containing ingredients that I figured you might be familiar with, ingredients that are commonly found in packaged food, and that was only half of the list that I have! If you do consume a lot of processed food, it will seem daunting to cut out these ingredients, and you may even suffer a few withdrawal-like symptoms (headache, nausea, fatigue, etc.), but once you become accustomed to eating whole food, you should notice a decrease in symptoms and an increase in your mobility, pain-free!

Grains

A couple of years ago, I remember reading (or hearing?) an explanation as to why we shouldn't eat grains, and that was along the lines of, 'If they fatten the cattle on grains, what do you think it's doing to you?' It was an a-ha moment for me, and it made sense; for those with autoimmune conditions, grains are a leading contributor to inflammation, particularly if leaky gut is involved, which, as we know, most autoimmune sufferers have. For lunch, every day that I was on shift at the local prison (yes, I was once a correctional officer), I would eat tuna, vegetables, rice, and halloumi. I never got tired of it, but what I did notice was that it failed to give me the energy I needed to get through a twelve-hour shift, due mostly to my urgent need for the bathroom within half an hour of eating. The reason why grains and pseudo-grains (amaranth, buckwheat, chia, and quinoa) present as a problem for autoimmune sufferers is due to a compound called lectin, which is discussed in the next food group. It also makes one question, if grains are such a powerhouse, nutritious food, why are the manufacturers constantly advertising that they've fortified this cereal or that bread? Why do they need to add minerals if the grain itself is already a superfood?

If you suspect you have an issue digesting grain, again I recommend elimination from the diet and healing and sealing the gut first, then reintroducing the offending grains one by one, keeping note of any symptoms that may present upon reintroduction. Like other food triggers, the purpose of elimination is so you can determine which foods incite inflammation. Few people can reintroduce some forms of rice and grains such as quinoa and couscous without issue; however, if you are not one of those people, please don't become despondent, as there are healthier alternatives out there, particularly ones that provide more vitamins and minerals than any food in the grain family does.

Nightshade Vegetables

I was sceptical when I first heard that nightshades may present an issue in immune-compromised people—since when does healthy food, vegetables at that, cause problems in the gut? Upon reflection, I did experience a few issues after eating a certain food, namely tomatoes. A work colleague would bring in little snack bags full of cherry tomatoes fresh off the vine, which I could not resist. I was eating a bag a day; they were delicious! I had just finished reading *Plant Paradox* by Steven Gundry, in which he describes that gluten may not be the only source of inflammation and that we should be looking at a plant-based protein called lectin as well, so maybe when these little snack bags of tomatoes appeared in the brew room, I was tempting fate, wanting to see if his theory was correct. After a couple of days of eating tomatoes, I woke to pain radiating through my ankles; it felt as though they'd been crushed with a sledgehammer. Turns out the good Doctor Gundry was onto something, and maybe one should not consume bag after bag of tomatoes! Other vegetables defined as nightshade include eggplant, capsicum, pumpkin, and potato (excluding sweet potato), common foods that most of us consume, so this is information to be aware of just in case you begin to notice that these vegetables and associated spices (paprika, cayenne pepper, etc) are affecting you.

Now I mentioned the reason that we have an issue digesting these foods is because of a carbohydrate-binding protein called lectin. There are many foods that contain this protein, some of which I have already mentioned; however, I will provide a brief overview here:

Pasta	Rice	Milk	Bread
Pastry	Tortillas	Flour	Crackers
Cookies	Cereal	Sugar	Sweeteners
Peas	Legumes	Soy	Tofu
Soy protein	Cheese	Ice cream	Oats
Rye	Corn		

See the pattern? The problem with lectin is that it could take years for disease to manifest. Again, you might experience a bit of discomfort and attribute it to something else, never making the connection between the protein and your symptoms. This is where keeping a food diary will benefit you; highlight any of the foods containing lectin—you might be shocked at just how much you consume.

Alcohol

'Listen to your body; it will tell you what it needs,' said my wise old owl (mother), although I don't think she meant that I should partake in a beer at 7.30 in the morning! When she walked into the lounge room and saw me doing exactly that (I was on holiday, and everyone knows there is such a thing as brekky beers while on holiday, duh), I reminded her of her statement, politely advising her that when I woke, my body said it wanted beer. She couldn't help but laugh.

However, for this protocol, I recommend that you do not consume beer or any other type of alcohol, particularly in the morning! Alcohol consumption irritates the gut, increasing the incidence of intestinal permeability and creating the perfect environment for unhealthy bacteria to develop. It was one of the first items I eliminated, along with gluten, and after a year or so of self-destructive binge drinking, removing it from my diet was an absolute necessity. Not only did I lose weight, but I felt clear-headed and focused as opposed to heavy and foggy. Italians will argue that alcohol has its benefits, and I agree, that there are some benefits to moderate consumption—it prevents Alzheimer's disease, reduces the risk of diabetes and cardiovascular disease, and may even reduce the risk of some cancers,[19] but for those with an autoimmune disease, a few Sunday sippers or after-work bevvies are probably doing more harm than good. Even a single drink for an immune-compromised individual can cause immense pain. Best stick to water until you heal your gut.

A Note about Meat

I alluded to meat not being entirely healthy earlier and would like to clarify that now. I love nothing more than a thick-cut rib-eye steak, slow cooked for eight hours, meat so tender that it falls apart upon plating. So why would I include it in my diet if it's not healthy? One must be a discerning shopper when it comes to purchasing cuts of meat, and I'm not just talking about talking about the high marble score rate.

First of all, most cattle and poultry are injected with hormones and antibiotics to fatten them up, keep them well, and rid them of parasites and other infections they may have acquired while in the yard. I wonder how long these medications remain in the animals and what effect any residual medication may have an autoimmune sufferer, particularly as it is not medication for humans.

---

[19] S Ballantyne, *The Paleo Approach,* Victory Belt Publishing, Canada, 2013.

Secondly, animals are fed on grains, which can be a trigger for autoimmune sufferers, as many cannot digest grains properly.

Thirdly, meat purchased from the supermarket is often packaged with water (to weigh heavier at the checkout—less meat for your money), which makes you wonder: what else do they do to the meat? There was talk a few years ago of chlorinated, acid-washed meat being sold in British supermarkets,[20] which made me question: is that something that could be happening here?[21] Makes your stomach curdle at the thought of eating acid-washed meat, doesn't it? That is why I allude to meat not being entirely healthy. The solution is simple—visit a reputable butcher and speak to them about their product. These guys love what they do, and they love it when customers take an interest. If you don't get a clear answer or they appear a bit cagey, find another butcher!

You can ask:

- Where does this meat come from?
- Is it an organic farm?
- Is it a biodynamic farm?
- Does the farm practice sustainable farming?
- Are the chickens genuinely free-range and cared for correctly?

---

[20] Reported by Sky News, 24/2/2020

[21] E Dormedy, Validation of Acid Washes as Critical Control Pointsin Hazard Analysis and Critical Point Systems, Journal of Food Protection, 2000, pp 1676-1680.

- What are the animals fed on? (I only eat meat that has been grass-fed, as it is easier for my gut to digest.)

Commercially cured meats (ham, salami, kabana) contain additives for preservation and should not be consumed on a daily basis.[22]

Symptoms of toxicity include difficulty breathing, headaches, and dizziness.

Fake meat is anything marketed to vegans/vegetarians that looks like meat but is not meat and is not even close to real food, as it is mostly chemical compounds processed together.

A quick word about foods that claim to lower cholesterol—the majority of these have been made in a laboratory, as the claim to lower cholesterol usually means they've subtracted the offending ingredient from the food (and often this ingredient is the one you need to eat!). If you are adhering to a whole food diet, I believe cholesterol would not be an issue, as you would be eating the food in its whole form as it is intended to be consumed.

---

[22] C O'Meara, *Lab To Table*, Changing Habits, Australia, 2019.

Awesome, Nourishing, Gut-loving, Nutrient-dense Foods

Fermented Food

Fermented foods have seen a resurgence in popularity over the last few years, as more people understand the importance of maintaining a diverse microbiome for optimal health. Fermentation is a process that helps prevent food spoilage, preventing harmful organisms from growing while good gut bacteria establish and providing active probiotic cultures and pre-digested, easy-to-absorb nutrients to food.

Daily consumption of fermented foods is understood to maintain the balance of intestinal flora, regulate the immune system and metabolic function, reduce the incidence of respiratory infections, improve bone, liver, body mass, and blood pressure indices, prevent diarrhea and constipation, and improve skin health. Additionally, a healthy gut microbiota and traditional dietary patterns, which include the consumption of fermented foods and beverages, may reduce the risk of anxiety and depression and control the stressors that can lead to cognitive dysfunction and neurodegenerative diseases.

Studies have compared the differences in the microbiome profiles of consumers and non-consumers, with the consumer profiles showing more of the lactobacillus strains of bacteria, known for preventing diarrhea, increasing production of short-chain fatty acids and relieving the symptoms of irritable bowel syndrome.[23] For us to keep our microbiome functioning optimally, we must give it good bacteria for it to thrive.

I love kimchi and make my own at home with cabbage, onion, carrot, garlic, chilli, ginger, tamari sauce, and water (you can omit the chilli, if you don't like spicy food). Other great fermented foods include yogurt (not the commercial variety that is full of added sugar), kombucha (again, not the supermarket variety, as it may contain added sugar; why not make your own?), sauerkraut (did you know that when fermented, cabbage contains twenty times the amount of vitamin C as fresh cabbage?!), kefir, and miso (yes, it is made from soybeans, but as it is fermented, it offers incredible benefits—regulates digestion, decreases cholesterol and blood pressure, prevents inflammation, relieves fatigue …). These foods contain a tonne of probiotics and prebiotics that are essential for good health.

---

[23] D Gille, Fermented Food and Non Communicable Chronic Disease: A Review, Nutrients, 2018.

Bone Broth

I cannot start the day without having a cup of bone broth; it is essential for healing the gut and providing the body with much-needed collagen to repair damaged cells and promote glowing skin, luxurious hair, and strong nails. Collagen, for those who may not have heard about it, is the tissue that holds everything together; it provides strength and structure and gives our skin its elasticity. Naturally, collagen production declines with age—hence the wrinkly, sagging skin and aching joints we lament as we take another lap around the sun.

The good news is that bone broth is easy to make; grab a huge stockpot (or slow cooker) and a couple of kilos of bones from any animal, cover with water, add vegetables or herbs for flavour, and cook for anywhere from four hours to forty-eight hours. When you've grown tired of waiting for it (I can be somewhat impatient), strain the liquid into a container and discard the bones and vegetables. You can also buy bone broth in powder and 'glue' form from health food shops. The vitamins, minerals, antioxidants, and amino acids the broth provides are numerous; however, the most important is probably glycine, which is important for synthesising DNA and RNA, wound healing, digestive health, memory, alertness, mood, relaxation, blood sugar regulation, and muscle repair.[24] There are amazing benefits from the consumption of broth!

---

[24] S Ballantyne, *The Paleo Approach*, Victory Belt Publishing, Canada, 2013.

Healthy Fats

The human brain is nearly 60% fat and therefore requires healthy fats to function at its best,[25] kind of like how your body is 60% water and needs this hydration to stay alive. Both saturated and unsaturated fats are needed for a healthy nervous system, energy production, liver function, immune system, the transport of essential fatty acids, the suppression of tumour growth, hormone production, and successful blood clotting. Fats also promote satiety, so you'll eat less than if you were consuming a predominantly carbohydrate-based diet. Healthy fat can be found in eggs, nuts, seeds, cold-pressed oils (olive, macadamia, avocado, walnut, etc), meat, fish, butter, liver, chicken, vegetables, fruits, grains, and legumes.

The most well-known fats, omega-3, and omega-6, are polyunsaturated fats that are necessary for the body to function. There's just one glitch—they cannot be produced in the body and must be obtained from food, hence why they are classified as essential fatty acids. Omega-3 is defined as anti-inflammatory and can assist with brain function, reduce cardiovascular risk, and prevent mental decline, while omega-6 is defined as pro-inflammatory, as high levels can induce joint pain, increase cardiovascular risk, and lead to other autoimmune disorders such as rheumatoid arthritis.[26]

---

[25] N Gedgaudas, *Primal Body, Primal Mind*, Healing Arts Press, Vermont, 2009.
[26] M Dei Cas, *Functional Lipids in Autoimmune Inflammatory Diseases*, International Journal of Molecular Science, 2020.

Both omega-3 and omega-6 are essential for repairing and maintaining health; however, those with certain conditions, such as lupus, need to ensure they are selecting the right source of fatty acid, as unbalanced levels of omega-6, can interfere with omega-3 metabolism.[27]

The Western diet has provided the perfect environment for autoimmune diseases to thrive. Many people are consuming too many omega-6 polyunsaturated fats in the form of vegetable oils, leading to the decline of health and flares in those who are immune-compromised. In contrast, the Mediterranean diet is associated with high levels of polyunsaturated fats beneficial to health.

Omega-3 can be found in wild-caught salmon, herring, sardines, mackerel, and cod liver oil, while omega-6 can predominantly be found in oils: sunflower, grapeseed, safflower, poppyseed, and vegetable (soybean and canola) oils. For optimal dietary consumption, balanced levels of both omega-3 and omega-6 can be found in whole animal products, the meat and fat from grass-fed and finished beef, lamb, and venison.

Offal (Organ Meat)

I feel as though a few of my readers just grimaced at the thought of eating offal. I hear you; I do not overly enjoy organ meat either (but don't tell my partner, because I slipped some liver into a lasagne sauce once and pretended

---

[27] A Manzel, Role of 'Western Diet' in Inflammatory Autoimmune Diseases, Current Allergy and Asthma Reports, 2014.

I loved it). For those who are not familiar with offal, I am referring to animal organs: liver, kidneys, heart, stomach, and brain. Yep, sounds gross and like something you might have never thought about cooking with, but it might surprise you to learn that offal is the most nutrient-dense, concentrated source of vitamins, minerals, amino acids, and healthy fats on the planet. Now, the experts will tell you that consuming organ meat increases blood cell production, supports organ function, and provides incredible iron and Vitamin A intake, but I understand it can be hard for some to bring themselves to eat it; after all, it doesn't factor in the standard Healthy Diet Pyramid, does it? I'll let you in on a secret. I cheat; I purchase powdered beef liver and heart capsules, crack them open, and sprinkle them on my food instead. Still reaping the benefits but without having to force it down like we did as kids when Mum confronted us with brussel sprouts!

Seafood and Shellfish

I love seafood, yet I probably do not eat it as often as I should. Fish and shellfish are among the richest sources of omega-3 fatty acids and contain a heap of vitamins and minerals such as calcium, phosphorous, fat-soluble vitamins A, D, E, and K, vitamin B12, iron, zinc, magnesium, copper, and potassium. Oh, and it also contains iodine and selenium, two very important minerals that, unfortunately, most people are deficient in. For autoimmune sufferers (well, pretty much everyone), it is recommended that fish be consumed at least three times a week, shellfish at least 1–2 times a week, and sea vegetables (think seaweed) at least once a week.

Vegetables

Yep, you may have hated them as a kid, but your mum was onto something when she piled them onto your plate and told you to eat them all—they are full of essential vitamins and minerals required for optimal health. And when it is recommended that your intake be between 8–10 servings a *day*, you will find yourself eating a variety for not only dinner and maybe lunch, but breakfast as well. This is not a new concept; people have been enjoying 'big breakfasts' for years, as this menu option generally contains tomato, spinach, and mushrooms among the eggs and bacon it is served with. Get used to enjoying a big breakfast at home and feel your body thank you.

A Word About Supplements

I took a lot of supplements when first diagnosed; some were mainstream supps such as fish oil, coenzyme Q10, vitamin D, vitamin E, calcium, iron, cranberry, and ginkgo biloba, while others were a little out of left field—deer antler, deer blood, bovine colostrum … Taking 'natural' supplements, I thought, would be better than taking medication prescribed by the doctor. Wrong. Mass-produced, store-bought supplements can do just as much damage as medication due to the manufacturing process. Often chemical solvents are used to extract the vitamins and minerals contained in the supplement, and it is bulked up with fillers of unknown origin or ingredient.[28] You need quite an investigative eye when faced with all those tablets and pills! The supplements I have now are those that come from real food and are produced by reputable companies/individuals (Changing Habits, Pete Evans, Tone Made, Ancestral Nutrition). On the days that I enjoy a smoothie in the morning, I like to give it a boost with a 'greens' powder and black seed oil, and as previously mentioned, I will crack open capsules of dehydrated organ meat and sprinkle it over my food.

An Even Briefer Note about Supplementation to Build Immunity Against Covid

Since the pandemic was announced, I've had a lot of people ask me about supplementation to assist them in building their immunity against Covid. In the beginning, I was eating an orange every day—an orange a day keeps the 'rona away! However, given the apparent ease of contracting and transmitting the virus, I began a precautional daily protocol that includes quercetin, N-acetyl-cysteine (NAC), vitamin D, vitamin A, zinc, glutathione, and pine-needle tea to give my immune system more of a fighting chance should I encounter the virus. Touch wood, two years on, and not even a sniffle. Note that this protocol will work for your regular cold-and-flu season too.

---

[28] C O'Meara, *Lab To Table*, Changing Habits, Australia, 2019.

What's in My Fridge and Pantry?

If you're anything like me, you enjoy a bit of a snoop, so you're probably wondering what I ate over the years as I sifted through the good, the bad, and the troublesome. As I've mentioned previously, if you consume something that doesn't agree with you, eliminate or substitute it. You'll notice I do consume some trigger foods (nightshades, as well as nuts and seeds, can be problematic for autoimmune sufferers); however, I do so with the knowledge they may cause a flare. Listen to your innate intelligence; your body will tell you what it wants.

MEAT & RELATED PRODUCTS	Beef	Lamb	Chicken
Turkey	Broth	Eggs	
SEAFOOD	Salmon	Whitefish, including shark	Sardines
Bugs	Crayfish	Prawns	Squid
VEGETABLES	Broccoli	Cauliflower	Zucchini
Capsicum	Carrot	Spinach	Onion—brown, red, spring, leek

Brussel sprouts	Pumpkin	Sweet potato	Lettuce
Celery	Cabbage	Squash	Asparagus
Artichokes			
FRUIT	Oranges	Apples	Strawberries
Blueberries	Blackberries	Peaches	Nectarines
Apricots	Plums	Avocado	Pineapple
Tomatoes	Cherries	Coconut	Watermelon
NUTS & SEEDS	Macadamias	Pecans	Walnuts
Brazil nuts	Cashews	Almonds	Hazelnuts
Sunflower seeds	Pepitas	Linseeds	Sesame seeds
Chia seeds			
FERMENTED FOOD/DRINK	Kimchi	Sauerkraut	Kombucha
DAIRY	Yoghurt	Cream	Raw milk
Cheese			
HERBS & SPICES	Garlic	Ginger	Oregano
Rosemary	Thyme	Sage	Turmeric
Paprika	Cumin	Coriander	Mint
Basil	Lemon balm	Parsley	Garam masala
Chilli flakes & powder	Pepper	Salt	
PANTRY ITEMS	Almond meal	Coconut flour	Tapioca flour
Cacao powder	Extra virgin olive oil	Coconut oil	Avocado oil
Rapadura sugar	Honey	Ghee	Coconut cream/milk
Olives	Gherkins		

Typical Meals Enjoyed in My House

I love to cook; the interest was always there, but when I was sick, I didn't have the enthusiasm for it as I do now. I usually follow a recipe first; then once I'm familiar with it, I add or delete as per my preference or that of my partner (who is quite a bland eater, whereas I do enjoy a bit of spice). My go-to recipe books include Pete Evans, Jamie Oliver, Changing Habits, any of the Women's Weekly Slow Cooking publications (altered to suit a Paleo/Keto approach), and any recipe found within the Autoimmune Protocol collection. I have also recently bought a Thermomix and have been experimenting a lot with their recipe platform, Cookidoo. My hope, once my vegetable garden is established, is to be making all of my food, i.e. condiments such as tomato paste, which I seem to go through by the truckload.

Note, some of these recipes do include nightshade vegetables and spices, so if you discover you cannot tolerate those foods, please remain cautious about including them in your diet, until you complete an elimination and reintroduction protocol.

BREAKFAST			
Hand-grenade egg bombs	Chia pudding	Smoothies	Scrambled eggs and kimchi
Bacon and egg frittata	Yogurt with berries	Granola	Stuffed omelette
LUNCH/DINNER			
Roast vegetable frittata	Ribolitta	Greek salad	Green salad with tuna or salmon
BLT wedges	Mexican bowls	Minestrone	Immune-boosting chicken soup
Stuffed chicken breasts	Zoodle Bolognese	Steak and veggies	Butter chicken with cauliflower rice
LCHF chicken kievs	Bacon-wrapped meatloaf	Slow-cooked roast meat	Hungarian ghoulash
Silverside with steamed greens	Chicken Caesar salad	Braised beef/ox cheeks	Eggplant lasagne
Coconut chicken curry	San choy bau	Shakshuka	Meatballs

Nutrition Action Steps

Step 1—Become Aware of What You Are Consuming

Keep a health diary/journal
Make note of everything you eat and drink, the way you feel afterward, any symptoms the food has produced, and how quickly these symptoms appeared.

What should your health journal include?

- food/drink intake
- symptoms and when these occur, i.e. before/after eating
- pain—the level of intensity during the day
- energy—what time do you experience the highest/lowest levels?
- exercise
- bowel movements—regular, sporadic, consistency, etc
- digestive issues—what time of day do these occur?
- medications taken

- supplements
- stressors
- overall mood
- any complementary therapies that may have been undertaken.

Learn to read and decipher the labels on packaged food

If you don't know what a particular item is, do some research (sourcing reputable health journals, such as *Nutrients*), and make some notes; more than likely, it will be something that your body should not be pressured to process. Avoid:

- additives
- preservatives
- numbers
- colours
- 'natural' flavours.

Know where your produce comes from

Shop for organic vegetables and fruit at your local farmers' market or visit roadside stalls. Speak to your local butcher and ask where they source their meat. Is it from an organic/biodynamic farm? Are the animals grass-fed? Are they given hormones or antibiotics? Your health is your responsibility, so do your homework!

Follow the leaders in holistic healthcare

I have mentioned some names of those who have helped

heal themselves and others of illness and disease; they have all undertaken extensive research and education about the effects diet and lifestyle have on human health and offer a range of information and products that expand upon what is contained within this book. Your health is your responsibility; be informed and educate yourself!

Step 2—Make Changes to Create Healthier Habits

One-ingredient pantry
As much as possible, try to store only products with one ingredient. Basics include spices, herbs, nuts, seeds, substitute flours, salt, and sugar. If this seems like a big task at the beginning, you can store items that have a couple of whole food ingredients, for example, organic tomato paste—99% tomatoes, sea salt. The key here is to notice what you keep in your pantry and how close those products are to real, whole food.

Follow a Paleo/Keto nutritional approach
Eat only real, whole food, as per the pyramid. There is a plethora of food for you to consume; as you will discover, the real struggle is getting past the belief that you need to consume bread, cereals, and grains. You will soon realise that the food you choose to eat from the Paleo/Keto Pyramid offers incredible health benefits. And remember to chew your food well to aid the digestion process.

Eliminate or substitute

The best method to determine what foods are causing a flare is elimination or substitution. I eliminated the following in their entirety:

- gluten and gluten-related products
- sugar
- soy and soy derivatives
- corn and corn derivatives
- grains
- dairy
- processed and fake meat.

If eliminating everything at the beginning is too much for you, take baby steps and eliminate one at a time or substitute for healthier choices, as discussed in this chapter. Ideally, you would want to undertake this step for at least a month, which should be sufficient time to observe a change in symptoms, and you might even find that you want to extend the duration of elimination to two or even three months, particularly if your health has improved dramatically.

Meal prep, meal prep, meal prep!

Most recipes can be prepared or cooked ahead of time. When a recipe stated it could not be frozen, I defied that note and put it in the freezer anyway! The more you stock your fridge and freezer with healthy food, the less you will be likely to snack on unhealthy food that may be available.

I'll be honest, living twenty minutes from a main town has also proved to be a great hindrance to just ducking down the street to get takeaway! I also implemented a rule that once our new house was built, no 'junk' food would be allowed. Those who have visited and enjoyed meals with us will undoubtedly tell you that there is usually a batch of freshly baked brownies on the kitchen bench. There it is, my naughty little not-so-secret addiction—I adore brownies; they are my favourite sweet treat. However, these are not filled with crap. I use almond meal in place of flour and dark chocolate chips in place of milk chocolate (and once you start looking, you'll find there are many 'treat' recipes using alternatives to the wheat flour, sugar, and chocolate).

Drink 2-3 Litres of Filtered Water Each Day

This might seem like a no-brainer, but funnily enough, people are still not drinking enough water! You might realise that you increase consumption in summer, as you tend to sweat more and use it in an attempt to cool yourself down, but in winter, it tends to go by the wayside. The good news is that many foods have a high water content (think cucumber, lettuce, celery, zucchini, watermelon, etc.), so if you include these foods in your daily consumption, then you are part way there! You can also increase your water consumption when you drink bone broth or herbal teas (sorry, beer is not a good option!).

Step 3—Supplement to Enhance Healing and Nurturing

Incorporate probiotics into daily eating

Some might argue that this should be included in Step 2; however, you cannot just start taking/eating probiotics, expecting them to heal your gut if you're still consuming inflammatory foods. By the time you get to Step 3, you have eliminated all the trigger foods and your gut has been given the chance to heal (this can take place in as little as 3–4 days; healing a leaky gut takes slightly longer, about 2–4 weeks), so now is the perfect time to load up on good bacteria. Make fermented foods part of your daily meal plan—it's easy if you love yogurt because you can start the day with yogurt and berries or nuts and seeds. Perfect!

Drink bone broth every day

I have previously discussed my love for bone broth, so you'll know by now that I cannot speak highly enough about it. A cup of broth each day will assist in continuing to heal and seal the gut, as well as all the other amazing health benefits that it offers. Drink this before (or even instead of) your morning coffee—you'll feel much more alert and energetic.

Introduce whole food supplements

I'm referring to dehydrated offal or greens powder, products that you might not be able to otherwise eat, or that you know you can get a huge whack of good stuff from in an obtainable amount—let's face it; it's easier to throw a teaspoon of thirty fruit and vegetables into a smoothie than it is to eat all of that in one day!

Step 4–Reintroduction

Ideally, you should give each nutrition step a significant amount of time for your body to detox and heal. This will also afford you the ability to recognise, and note, the changes that occur. Reintroduction of food happens at the completion of all steps after you have noticed a considerable improvement in your symptoms, as this will provide a more accurate representation of which foods do not serve you. I gave the elimination process a couple of months before I considered reintroducing foods and only did so if I felt it would not result in a flare. If I experienced any discomfort, the food was quickly removed, and I focused on further healing of my gut. You may find that the reintroduction phase for some foods requires more time—that's okay. Where you are at today will be different from where you are, in a month's time, or a week, for that matter. The key is to have sealed your gut as much as possible so that the foods you do reintroduce can be acceptably tolerated. Choose the foods that are least likely to cause a flare or major setback to begin with, then consider those that you may have had issues with previously. If you experience a flare, eliminate the food again, concentrate on further healing of the gut, and try reintroduction again at a later date, if you wish. Some people like to try reintroduction a couple of times to accurately decide whether the food can be tolerated or to eliminate the offending food altogether.

Lifestyle and Environment

The best six doctors anywhere, and no-one can deny it, are sunshine, water, rest, air, exercise and diet.

—Wayne Fields,
author of *What the River Knows*

Once you have conquered the diet component of the autoimmune warrior protocol, it is time to look at your surroundings. What might be causing inflammation and pain? Do you use household chemicals for cleaning? Are you experiencing more stress? Are you getting adequate sleep, or is your sleep broken? What exercise are you doing? What's your level of exposure to electromagnetic fields? My life was in a state of chaos when I was diagnosed. I was grieving for my mum, I was repairing my relationship with my father, I was indulging in self-sabotaging behaviour, I did not respect myself, I was not eating well, I was abusing alcohol, and I was angry with the world. All of these factors contributed to my worsening condition, and the removal of these factors contributed to a much healthier disposition.

Stress

We'll start with the impact of stress. It's very easy to get into a negative mindset when you're living with chronic pain, particularly if you're young, as I was; 'Why me?' is a question often asked. 'I have jobs to do, kids to look after, homework to help with, bills to pay, a house to maintain, meals to prepare and cook, elderly parents to care for, a life to live. I can't be sick. I can't do this. I'm a failure.' While you're telling yourself this, you're increasing the stress on your body, and unfortunately, this is compounding your health issues. Not only are you putting pressure on your mental health, but you are causing great harm to your internal organs as well.

Illness and disease feed off stress, just as it feeds off unhealthy food. I was conscious that when I felt my heart rate increase and I was becoming grumpier with those around me, I was putting my body under undue stress, exacerbating my symptoms, and I needed to find a way to calm myself down. Often, my answer was to read. Yes, it would not provide a solution to the stressor, but it did give me time to slow down, clear my mind, and relax before confronting the problem. I also love to walk, get out into nature, and ground myself back to the earth. Recently I have begun to meditate, which is also an effective way to deal with stress. Meditation is a beautiful way to focus on what there is to be grateful for and to turn off the chaos in your mind.

Exposure to chemicals—Cleaning Products, Skincare, Pesticides

Chemicals are everywhere in our environment. I believe more people are aware of the dangers and have started making changes within the house and workplace to reduce their toxic load. If you're interested in knowing what you're ingesting or absorbing, PubChem is a great resource for researching the ingredients of common household chemicals; it's quite frightening. Once you learn something, you can't unlearn it, and there were many times I felt physically nauseous at what I had brought into my surroundings.

As I stated earlier when discussing the glyphosate in Roundup, these chemicals may be deemed 'safe', but they are still toxic, even in small quantities, and I can almost guarantee that not everyone will be wearing full PPE in the administration of these chemicals. Over the last two years, with the threat of coronavirus present in our lives, we have been encouraged to sanitise. In my opinion, this is one of the worst things you can do, as it kills off the good bacteria that build your immune system. Practicing good hygiene is one thing, but weakening your immune system only leads to vulnerability to infections. Many chemicals that are used for cleaning are absorbed through the skin or inhaled through the nose and mouth, causing damage to muscles, joints, lungs, heart, blood cells, kidneys—basically every organ in the body. It may seem overwhelming to rid yourself of these toxins, and you might not be able to eradicate all of them, so focus on what you can control. Swap your household cleaning products for vinegar, water, and essential oils. A multipurpose cleaner scented with orange is one of the most popular cleaning products sold in the supermarket; why not make your own with water and orange essential oil? Or eucalyptus, tea tree, lemon … All very effective, and instead of receiving a synthetic hit of perfume, you're inhaling the real thing. Pretty simple, huh? You'll probably find your concoction lasts longer, too, as you will be less liberal with the spray for the same result—a clean benchtop. You can also apply the use of oils to products such as insect spray. Citronella is one of the ingredients in chemical sprays; why not remove the chemicals and use a combination of citronella, orange, and lemon? I'm sure I'm just reinforcing what you already know because that was exactly how I felt; it makes sense.

That's all well and good for cleaning products, but what about skincare? You probably haven't given much thought to what goes on your skin, and maybe you don't want to check the ingredients because you love your make-up and you'll be mortified, so just let me say, this is the elephant in the room that needs to be addressed. When I was in my twenties, I worked at Target in the cosmetics department—plain Jane me. Foundation and mascara were about the extent of my foray into the make-up scene. Until a rep for Revlon asked how I can be expected to sell the product if I don't use it. Well, that changed everything. Given my meagre wage, I told him I couldn't afford to kit myself up every day, even with a 5% discount. So, when he said to me, 'Make a list of everything you'd like, and next time I'm down, I'll bring full-sized samples with me,' I jumped at the chance to get involved in the art of face painting! He stocked my drawers with about $400 (RRP) worth of goodies, and suddenly, my eyelids were all shades of pink, purple, blue, green, and brown. I was drawing black or brown lines to accentuate my eyes, and I was wearing light shades of lipstick. And it wasn't just my face that was painted; my nails got the rainbow treatment as well! And let's not forget the body wash, body lotion, cleansers, toners, moisturisers, and deodorants … Wow, talk about a toxic load!

While I may not have been using all those items when I was diagnosed, the years and years of accumulation led to years of pain and inflammation. Eventually, I stopped using make-up, mainly because it was too exhausting to apply, and just focused on hygiene products. But even that was causing damage. Deodorant is one of the worst products due to it containing aluminium, and where do you roll deodorant? Right over a lymph node, into your circulatory system, ready to disrupt your hormones. You can see how sick you can become, and that's just one product. Like food, skincare products are best when they are as organic as possible. I love to use the Twenty8 skincare range, created by Kim Morrison, or if you want to make your own, drop some essential oils into a carrier oil for a lovely moisturiser.

Exposure to EMFs

As technology advances, so does our exposure to radiation from EMFs, and that can have a huge effect on our body, including disruption of hormones, infertility, brain damage/tumours, gut issues, cancer, mental health disorders, oxidative stress, etc. I heard a great saying the other day—'Cell phones are the cigarettes of the 21st century'—because they are addictive and detrimental to health. Some EMFs, such as sunlight, are produced in nature and important to health, while others are man-made and can be attributed to serious health complications.

Examples of man-made EMF sources include computers, mobile phones, wireless smart home devices (smart locks, Google Home, or Alexa), smart meters, powerlines, electrical wiring, and electrical appliances. Each EMF has its own frequency (the number of waves that pass through a fixed point in a second) and can be classified into two groups, ionizing and non-ionizing radiation, both of which can disrupt the structure of cellular functions within the body. The low-frequency non-ionizing radiation emitted from wireless devices, once considered relatively safe, is now being investigated to assess the effect on biological processes such as hormone production, synthesis of RNA and DNA, and immune responsivity. Studies have shown exposure to the radiation emitted from mobile phones caused significant DNA damage in 56% of cases examined as well as altering the permeability of the blood-brain barrier, triggering neural disorders and causing damage to various parts of the brain. There is also strong evidence to support EMFs' role in infertility, with many studies revealing an increase in foetal abnormalities, reduced sperm motility, and destruction of tissue and cells in the ovaries, uterus, and fallopian tubes. Continued regular exposure to EMFs can lead to fatigue, headaches, impaired cognitive function, poor concentration, anxiety, changed metabolic process, joint and muscular pain, and stress.[29]

Look around you. What electronic equipment is in the room? In my study, as I write this, I have a laptop, my partner has a laptop, there is a multifunction printer, several power points with USB ports, my mobile phone, a wireless mouse, computer monitor, security system base station, and a Bluetooth speaker. Sounds about average for a home office, right? All of these items are emitting EMFs, and while they may be in small quantities because there are multiple appliances, it increases the radiation load on my body. Consider your kitchen. Lots of power points for all those appliances, a food processor, microwave, fridge, oven, dishwasher. More load on the body. Do you have a smart TV? Do you have solar panels? Do you have security cameras, as I do? Is there a mobile phone tower nearby? What electrical items are contained in your workplace? By now, your head is probably swimming and you're probably thinking this is an insurmountable task. *There's no way I can clear all those EMFs from my life.* And you'd be correct.

---

[29] J Mercola, *EMF*D*, Hay House, Australia, 2020.

You won't be able to get rid of every single point of radiation, but you can reduce the emissions received by the body. I will include some points on how you can limit your exposure to EMFs in the Lifestyle Action Steps.

While the aforementioned contributed to my weakened state of health, listed below are the therapies that I found enabled me to regain some energy, reduce joint and muscular pain, and begin to live a normal, sociable life again.

Holistic Therapies

Chiropractic

I was extremely fortunate to have been brought up by a chiropractor. From an early age, I learned about the human body and how it functioned; I even assisted Dad with patients that required specific cranial adjustments. Whenever I had a biology question, Dad would hand me his copy of *Gray's Anatomy* to find the answer (sometimes this would be accompanied by a dictionary so I could decipher the anatomical words; in hindsight, that's probably where my love of research began). While Dad may have been sceptical about my condition initially, I maintained chiropractic care but would ask him to focus on certain points or use an activator if I was unable to withstand touch. I held a lot of tension in my stomach and experienced nausea pretty much daily, which can be quite debilitating. I discovered there was a fine line between nausea and hunger—if I didn't eat at the right time, the nauseous sensation grew, or I would experience pain, just underneath my diaphragm, which, until I knew better, I interpreted as hunger. I quickly learned that the pain indicated I was unable to release waste and the only way to alleviate the pain was a chiropractic technique applied to my stomach. Of course, chiropractic adjustments might not be for everyone, but for me, I couldn't imagine not continuing with chiropractic care. I just knew it was what my body needed.

Massage
I'm sure I just heard a few readers gasp at the suggestion that someone touch their pain-riddled body. When you are experiencing a flare, there's nothing worse than having a deep-tissue massage. Hell, even a relaxation massage can feel like someone is dragging a rake across your back. But if your flare is mild and you find the perfect masseuse with the lightest touch, like I did (after many excruciating, crippling appointments), massage is incredibly beneficial in that it helps to stimulate the lymphatic system and gets those blood cells moving freely again.

Acupuncture
I was already well when I discovered acupuncture, so I look upon it as necessary for maintenance care. For someone who is just starting on their health journey, I would definitely recommend acupuncture, mainly because there is no pain in the delivery of inserting the needles, which allows healing without experiencing further pain, as one would with a massage treatment.

Floating

Floating is one of the most restful activities you can do. Not only do you feel as though you've had a solid eight hours of sleep in one hour, but it relaxes the entire body, decompressing your spine and every joint in the body. Brilliant for soothing chronic pain, strengthening the immune system, and relieving stress. Hands down one of the best treatments for autoimmune sufferers.

Additional Therapies I've Researched But Not Yet Tried

Kinesiology combines muscle monitoring with the principles of traditional Chinese medicine to assess energy and body functions. Kinesiology can be used for a range of issues and symptoms including pain, sports performance, weight management, detoxification, fatigue, learning difficulties, and behavioural problems.

Reiki is a Japanese technique for stress reduction and relaxation that promotes healing based on the idea that an unseen life-force energy flows through us. Reiki treats the person as a whole, focusing not only on the body but emotions, mind, and spirit as well.

Hyperbaric oxygen therapy involves breathing oxygen in a pressurised environment, increasing the amount of oxygen your blood can carry and speeds up the recovery and healing process.

I don't expect you to undertake all these therapies, as that could prove quite costly, and we're not all millionaires! Select the ones that appeal or that you feel you will benefit the most from and start there. Give any therapy that you try at least a couple of visits and track any changes you may experience, or symptom relief, in your journal. If you find after a couple of sessions that the therapy is not working for you, discontinue and try something else; there is no point sticking with something that does not benefit you.

Use of Essential Oils

We've altered our eating habits to include real food, and we've swapped out our cleaning products for oils—oils from which the ingredients are found in nature. But these beauties have an array of uses, not just cleaning. Our ancestors would use oils for medicinal purposes and healing. They can also be used to improve our mental disposition. Memories, both good and bad, often come with an associated smell. Every morning, I do a body boost ritual (more on this later) utilising essential oils in a carrier oil with magnesium spray. I have rollerball mixtures to roll on during the day for focus, clarity, energy, relaxation, etc. I have a diffuser going in the study while I work, one going in the open-plan family room and kitchen, and one at night-time when I go to sleep. I make my bath salts with essential oils to reduce inflammation, stimulate muscle recovery, and invoke relaxation. Honestly, oils are used pretty much every hour of every day in my house.

When my partner began to get sick about twelve months ago (no, it was not Covid, just the common cold), I boiled some water, put some drops of eucalyptus, tea tree, clary sage, and lavender in the bowl, and told him to stick his head over it and inhale. His congestion was gone within a day; now he calls my oils 'that witchcrafty stuff', but he uses them nonetheless, and I have overheard him speaking to others about the benefits of oils. It's natural, and it works!

Sleep

Sleep is underestimated by many people. Unfortunately, for those living with an autoimmune disease, whole-body fatigue is common, and you would assume this exhaustion would make it easy to fall asleep. Well, that is not always the case. There were many nights when I would wander off to bed, hardly able to keep my eyes open anymore, only to have them spring wide awake the moment my head hit the pillow. What the … ? Frustrating, to say the least, as it often meant during the day (and usually at work), I struggled to stay awake. My friend (you know, the boss) recognised the signs of me fading throughout the day and very kindly, one day, while we were working an outage at one of the power stations, suggested that I take a nap. He locked the door to the ATCO hut so no-one could disturb me, and I was able to get the rest I needed. I was so exhausted that I fell asleep instantly, and the floor in those huts is bloody hard!

In her book, *Paleo Principles*, Sarah Ballantyne lists the percentages connecting lack of sleep with the risk of developing autoimmune disease—systemic lupus erythematosus goes up 81%, rheumatoid arthritis goes up 45%, and if you are obese or have diabetes, your risk of autoimmune disease doubles. Oh, and let's not forget our shift workers, who, with their erratic sleep schedules, have a 50% higher risk of autoimmune disease than those colleagues who work a normal 9–5 day. Good sleep is necessary to give the body a chance to recover and regenerate, and it is essential for optimal health, so I have included some action steps at the end of the chapter if you're tackling a bit of autoimmune-related insomnia.

Exposure to the sun

Yes, you need to expose yourself to the sun; no, it doesn't need to result in you getting burnt! You only need 10–15 minutes each day (preferably before 10 am) to help you build a tolerance to sunlight exposure and for your body to utilise what it has absorbed and convert it into Vitamin D. The other benefit of the sun is that it improves your mood—who doesn't feel better when the day is beautiful, the birds are chirping, the sky is bright blue, and the sun is shining? Exactly. Difficult to be frustrated by the world when mother nature turns on the 'beauty'. You may also find that you sleep better, as your body will be able to produce melatonin, a hormone that regulates the sleep-wake cycle.

Movement

As an autoimmune sufferer, the last thing on your mind is movement. *It's painful, I'm limited as to what I can do,* and *I'm utterly exhausted from getting through the day; how on earth am I going to fit physical activity into my schedule?* These are all thoughts that cross your mind. I've been there; I've thought all those things and more. Yes, it is bloody painful taking that first step, and yes, you might not get far, and yes, you might end up even more fatigued, but you need to incorporate some sort of movement into your day. It doesn't have to be overly strenuous; as I stated before, I could barely walk around the block. But bit by bit, as I improved my diet, my capacity to complete exercise also strengthened. As my blood cells began to move more freely, so did my body, and before long, I was walking up to 10 km plus every day. Once I got my mojo back, I investigated other modalities of movement.

I found yoga to be incredible—it stretches your limbs without being too taxing on the body and teaches you about the importance of breath and the connection between mind and body. And although I resemble one of those inflatable dolls (you know, the ones that are used outside businesses to gain your attention) flapping about in the wind, I love to dance. So, when I spend the weekend in the kitchen doing my meal prep, I'd put some music on and sway or jump around, depending on the genre of the song.

The temperature in the sauna
My secret weapon throughout those years was undoubtedly my thrice-weekly visits to an infrared sauna. Now you might think that's cheating, but I consider it to be resourceful. You see, my autoimmune disease flares when it's cold.

My fingers are crippled, my body frozen, and my mind blank; I simply don't function in the cold. In the heat, it's a different story. I thrive. So, it made sense that I should give the sauna a go. It was a complete detox for my body. While I sat there reading, I sweat out the toxins that were giving me grief. I oxygenated my blood cells. I improved my skin tone. And I regained the use of my arthritically challenged fingers. This treatment was what enabled me to hike kilometre after kilometre. Many gyms and health-related facilities have infrared saunas; however, if you are not comfortable attending there (I am not a gym junkie at all), you can do what I did and buy one for yourself (my partner nearly flipped when I came home from taking the dog swimming with a three-person sauna and setting it up in the lounge room!). Models range from a few hundred to a few thousand, depending on size, or, as I've recently discovered after having to sell my beloved sauna (built a massive forty-square-metre house only to find out there's no room for the sauna), you can pick up a sauna blanket for anywhere between $400–800. They're great because they're fully portable, so you don't have to leave the house to get your fix, and they're a cost-effective solution if you are a little unsure about entering the sauna space.

Bathing

While on the subject of heat, another treatment used in conjunction with the sauna visits (although this modality was a prelude to the sauna) was bathing in therapeutic water.

Admittedly, I began in the volcanic water of Rotorua, New Zealand, but you can bathe in any water and it will be of benefit, especially if it contains anti-inflammatory salts. I wouldn't have believed it unless I experienced it for myself; it seemed such a crazy notion—bathing could help alleviate the pain?! Absolutely! When I first landed in Rotorua, I could barely bend my knees, and I was doing my hair upside down because my shoulder felt torn—every time I tried to raise my arm, it felt like bone grating against bone. Ouch. My movement was incredibly limited. But then I bathed for an hour or so in the Priest Pools at the Polynesian Spa (named after three priests who discovered that bathing in this volcanic water with a specific chemical composition alleviated their arthritic aches and pains) and the next morning, I was jumping out of bed and throwing my arms above my head. It was instant relief for a body that had struggled for two years. I made a promise to myself then that I would return every year, even if I didn't feel like I needed it—at worst, it was a mini holiday; at most, it would keep the MCTD at bay.

Participation in rituals

Rituals are a great expression of self-love; it shows you respect yourself enough to allocate the time to do something positive that is just for you (no kids, no pets, no boss, no husband or wife—just *you*). It doesn't have to be elaborate; your ritual could be something as simple as meditating for five minutes every morning, focusing on your breath work, or undertaking a body boost (credit to Kim Morrison, founder of Twenty8, for this simple, beautiful gem of a process that sets the tone and intent for the day). I admit I do cheat and purchase the full range of Twenty 8 body boost oils; however, you can make your own using a carrier oil, a few drops of essential oil, and magnesium spray. Starting at the feet, put a few drops in the palm of your hands and rub the oil into your feet. Consider your intent for the day, repeat a positive affirmation in your mind or speak it out loud, and allow yourself to appreciate your body. Embrace the positive flow of emotion as you work your way up your body, massaging the oil into your skin, inhaling the perfume of the oils, and notice how that process and scent lift your mood. You might even consider putting together a rituals kit—body boost, affirmations to repeat, gratitude journal, diffuser, inspirational quotes, etc—that you can reflect upon daily. Or you might like to spend a few minutes working on a vision board. Find what works for you, implement it daily, and notice how it improves your approach to each day and life in general.

Connection

For a while there, after my diagnosis, I would make plans with friends, then cancel, or, as Facebook reminds me, I used to beg people to come over and bring food with them (not surprisingly, no-one ever did). You see, I would make those plans in the morning hours, when I was up and mobile and thinking I could do something productive rather than binge *The Good Wife* on Netflix (although it was a great show). But come mid-afternoon, I was exhausted and heading home for a nap. Of course, my friends would get shitty because I'd cancelled plans—again—but how could I explain to them that I was physically and emotionally spent? Peer pressure is big in this country, and if you don't look sick, people assume you're a healthy individual who can participate in all the activities they do. So, I became a bit of a hermit. This way of coping, I do not recommend. We need connection, we need human contact. If I were a more persuasive person, I would have explained how I was feeling and asked them if they could sit with me, watch a movie, and solve the world's problems!

You see, just as eating our vegetables is essential for good health, so are our social connections. It has been proven across many studies that people who feel more connected have lower levels of anxiety and depression, less inflammation, higher levels of confidence and self-esteem, greater empathy, the ability to regulate emotions, and less antisocial behaviour and suicide ideation. I may have only had one good friend on board who understood what I was going through, but that was enough at the time. If you find you don't have friends who make the effort to understand or to spend time with you, look for a support group. I joined a couple, one based in the UK, and one based in the USA, and honestly, it was great talking to people who were going through the same thing, who didn't brush me off when I asked a question or get grossed out when I mentioned that I had experienced unusual female-related symptoms due to my condition.

I am also of the firm belief that having a four-legged companion works wonders; it's hard to be so consumed with your pain when they lay their head on your lap and stare at you with big brown eyes, pleading for love—just be careful if you have a puppy like mine that enjoys eating faeces and thinks it's funny to try and lick you afterward. At diagnosis, I had an older male labrador who happened to be diagnosed with arthritis at about the same time, and we would often be seen commencing our healing journey with a short and very slow walk around the neighbourhood.

Currently, I have two labradors, male and female, and two German short-haired pointers, male and female, and they all have their own unique personality. There is honestly nothing better than being on the receiving end of their unconditional love.

Lifestyle Action Steps

Step 1—Reduce Toxic Load

Limit exposure to EMFs

We cannot eliminate all EMFs from our environment, but we can make simple adjustments to daily living that will limit our exposure, as Joseph Mercola writes in *EMF*D:*

- Don't sleep with your mobile phone in the bedroom.
- Connect computers with an ethernet cable as opposed to going wireless.
- Use Bluetooth sparingly, and try not to use it in the car if possible.
- Don't hold your phone to your head when taking phone calls; this emits radiation directly to your brain—scary stuff! Use corded headphones or use the speaker function.
- Install filters designed to reduce electricity.
- Take a break from the computer every hour; go outside, take your shoes off, and ground into the earth.
- Turn the wi-fi off, at night, if possible.

- Don't put your phone in your back pocket or bra, as these areas are in direct line with reproductive organs.
- Heat food in the oven instead of the microwave.
- Ensure adequate intake of magnesium; this is essential for the stability of cell function, RNA and DNA synthesis, and cell repair.
- Ensure adequate intake of Vitamin E; this has the potential to prevent adverse effects of EMF exposure by improving the regenerative cycle, increasing elasticity and the body's tolerance.

Ditch the chemical-laden cleaning products

This is not a difficult step to take, and you will notice the effect on your health immediately. If you're doubtful, spray some chemicals around, breathe them in, and feel the burn in your lungs and nasal cavity. Now make up a spray bottle of essential oils and water, spray them around, and breathe them in … Feel the difference? Not only do these products clean your house, but they smell great and do not cause you harm.

Rethink your skincare

By now, you're probably more aware of what's going in and on your body; you may even have started looking at labels. If you wouldn't eat something you can't pronounce, why would you put it on your skin? Choose a natural, organic brand that is reputable, like Twenty8, Sodashi, or Bare by Bauer, or, as I suggested, a few drops of essential oil into a carrier oil makes for a lovely moisturiser.

Step 2—Rest to Heal

Manage stress

When life gets overwhelming, find something that calms you down and focus on that until you feel as though you can tackle the problem without getting worked up. You might choose to meditate, perform breathwork, or go for a walk, while others might prefer to journal or do some mindfulness colouring. It doesn't matter what the activity is; it only matters that you find a way to deal with the stressor before it eats you alive.

Sleep

The best time for our body to heal is when we sleep, so we must ensure that we are doing everything we can to get adequate sleep every night and wake to feel refreshed and ready to take on the world. To do this, we should:

- aim for eight hours every night
- go to bed at the same time
- avoid drinking alcohol and caffeine and stop eating three hours before bedtime
- indulge in a relaxing bath with some drops of lavender essential oil and Epsom salts
- have a diffuser going with a relaxation blend of oils (I enjoy good old lavender but also diffuse mandarin, ylang-ylang, marjoram, bergamot, chamomile, neroli, and melissa)
- listen to meditative music
- avoid technology before bed; read a book instead!

Step 3—Move to Thrive

Undertake gentle exercise

I'm not talking about completing marathons (I couldn't think of anything more taxing than running for 42 km; apologies to my marathon-competing friends!), but some form of gentle exercise to raise the heart rate a little and get your blood cells moving freely will do you a world of good. Walking, swimming, and yoga are great, although if you are used to more strenuous activities, it may take a bit of time to adjust to the slower pace. Once you begin to feel better, you could incorporate some weights; small dumbbells are great for reinstating muscle tone, or you might prefer to take in nature while hiking with a backpack, as I did. Again, this is a case of finding what works for you. If you feel an activity is no longer serving you, find another activity. Maybe the thought of a block of time dedicated to exercise is not your groove, but implementing little movements throughout the day is something you can achieve. Park your car at a reasonable distance away from work or the shops and walk to your destination. Take a walk in the park during your lunch break. Shoot some hoops with the kids if you are able. Do some gardening, water the plants, pull some weeds, or do a little digging. Or, as my friend does because she loathes walking, dance around the kitchen while you're preparing meals—it's fun and doesn't feel like exercise!

Step 4—Connect to Mind and Body

Try a complementary therapy

Consider one that involves a holistic approach to health and learn about the philosophy behind the therapy. Think about which therapy may best suit your needs, one that would work well with your condition. If you are sensitive to touch, as I was, you might like to try floating, acupuncture, Reiki, or kinesiology.

Spend time with family and friends

Motivation and energy are non-existent in the beginning stages of managing an autoimmune condition; just the thought of spending time with others is draining, but you must make time to grow those connections. If you feel overwhelmed with a social situation, speak to your loved ones and explain how you're feeling; you might be surprised at their level of understanding. The right people will stick around; these are the people you don't have to put on airs and graces for, those you can be yourself around, those who will just sit still with you without the need for chatter.

Indulge in a ritual

This gives you the time to focus solely on yourself. That's not to say your other commitments (family, work) are not important, but you cannot fill from an empty cup. Look after yourself first and foremost so you can be present when you are needed by others. Take the time to show gratitude for all that you are surrounded by: the beauty, love, opportunities, pleasures, memories, nature …

Mindset

You are the storyteller of your life; make sure it's creative.

—Anon

I believe this protocol was successful for me because I remained positive, kept an open mind, and questioned everything. I was not prepared to live a life of negativity, nor was I going to allow others to control how I dealt with my health. I was, and still am, willing to try new, and sometimes what others perceive as crazy, ideas in the quest to eradicate my disease. You can change your diet, and you'll notice a difference; you can eliminate or reduce as many chemicals as possible, and you'll notice a difference; you can start moving, and you'll notice a difference, but none of it will go the distance if you don't improve your mindset as well. Consider the law of attraction. If you consistently have negative thoughts about your situation, particularly when the pain takes over daily living, the universe can only respond to that emotion, and you will feel as though your life is at a stalemate; there will be no progression to move you out of the struggle. But if you project positivity and visions of overcoming your diagnosis or having success in other areas of your life, the universe will respond to your positive vibrational energy and reward you in kind.[30] I recently read *Manifesting Matisse* by Dr Michelle K Nielsen and have to say, I felt it was an absolute game-changer. I wish I had known about it when I was ill; I may have been able to speed up my recovery through the process of manifestation! The book follows the author's application of the law of attraction to manifest her son's healing from developmental delay and neurological damage, explained through a ten-step process that is both simple and fun to complete. The summation is that you are the creator of your life; what you manifest and project to the universe is what you will receive.[31] If you are interested in the spiritual world and developing the skillset to bring your dreams to fruition, then this is a fantastic book to get started with.

My parents used to say, 'Everything happens for a reason.' However, after reading *Manifesting Matisse* (and then *Ask and It Is Given* by Esther Hicks, *The Secret* by Rhonda Byrne, and *The Artist's Way* by Julia Cameron, because I'm a nerd and love to learn), I believe that these things happen because we have projected our deepest desires out into the

---

[30] E Hicks, *The Law of Attraction*, McPherson's Printing Group, Australia, 2006.
[31] M Nielsen, *Manifesting Matisse*, USA, 2008.

universe and the universe is responding to our thoughts. Let's use my situation as an example. I wasn't happy in my day-to-day job and had been contemplating putting all my energy into my health-coaching business, but to forego a regular wage is quite a daunting prospect, so I persevered with my job—until the state government-mandated Covid vaccinations for the industry I worked in. Having now read my story, and undergoing your own struggles, you may understand my apprehension in getting the vaccine; there was no guarantee that the vaccine would not provoke an autoimmune-enhanced response in my body, and I simply couldn't risk my health and undo all the work I'd put in over the last ten years. I chose not to get the vaccine, which ultimately led to my employment being terminated. Strangely enough, I thought I'd be a little more stressed at the thought of not having a job, but I was calm, as though I instinctively knew that I would be alright. The universe had observed my unhappiness in my vocation and had structured events to direct me onto the path I am meant to be on. I felt at peace for the first time in a long time; everything just felt right.

Pre-MCTD diagnosis, I was always a spiritual person—typical Pisces nature, very empathetic, emotional, dreamy, and connected to Spirit. However, I feel at times, I lost my way and didn't listen to my intuition or acknowledge the guidance that was in plain sight. I feel the events over the last few months have led me back to my spiritual self. I found myself at a self-care retreat that reaffirmed I was on the right path, and from that, I began to devour content relevant to connecting with Spirit, or, as some refer to it, Source Energy. This information is along the same lines as *Manifesting Matisse,* teaching how to ask, visualise, and receive what you have manifested. It might sound a bit like voodoo to those who have not ventured down this road before, and that's okay. One day, something will happen; you'll hear a podcast that mentions a person or a book, like the one that I have mentioned here, and before you know it, you'll find yourself searching for more information. The universe gives you what you put out there, but it also gives you what you need at exactly the right time, as it has with me.

The world is limitless, abundant and strangely accommodating.

— Florence Scovel Shinn

Manifest

I've said it before, and I'll say it again: you do not have to become your diagnosis! Many think that they receive attention when they play the victim, but this is sending the wrong message to the universe. If you think of yourself as ill, you will remain ill. If you speak of yourself as ill, you will remain ill. Visualise yourself as a healthy individual. You wake in the morning feeling refreshed, you enjoy a hearty breakfast, you can start work on time, and you are energised throughout the day. You can enjoy a walk with friends after work, you dance in the kitchen as you prepare a nourishing meal for your family, and you feel satisfied that you've had a productive day free from pain and other debilitating symptoms. Now think about yourself as an ill person, struggling to wake each day, fighting off nausea, and battling to stay awake at work. You have little social contact with friends because you're too tired to catch up or in too much pain to exercise. You reach for the nearest convenience food because you don't have the energy to cook, and you have a glass of wine in an attempt to numb the pain, but all it leaves you with is brain fog and a restless night's sleep. Which scenario do you prefer? While I've only just developed my understanding of the manifestation process, I have always been a dreamer and so have been unknowingly carrying out manifestations as I grow.

I've been somewhat apprehensive about including the following experience; however, it is relevant to the nature of this book, so I will share what I considered at the time to be a fangirl moment, but I now realise I likely manifested the whole scenario as though I were writing the script for my life to play out. Since I was a teenager, I had loved the band, *Matchbox 20*; they were huge when I was growing up, always featuring in the Top 40, and I remember receiving their hit, *Unwell*. on CD single for my sixteenth birthday. When I became ill, a friend told me that they had listened to a song by Rob Thomas called *Her Diamonds*, in which he spoke about his wife's battle with chronic illness. It quickly became my theme song. That song reminded me that illness doesn't discriminate; this guy was worth millions, yet he felt useless watching his wife in pain, knowing there was nothing he could do to help her. Every time I felt that MCTD was getting the better of me, I would listen to that song and know that I was not alone—what I wouldn't give to talk to Mari, or Rob, about her experience and how she managed to get through the days.

Twelve months on, I found myself working in Melbourne, living in residence at a swanky hotel on Chapel Street, and overheard that *Matchbox* 20 was staying in that very hotel; what were the chances of that happening? The guy whose song got me through some of the worst times of my life, the guy whose wife had been diagnosed with an autoimmune condition similar to mine, was staying in the same hotel as me?! I was in overdrive. I told everyone I worked with that if I had the chance to meet Rob Thomas (squeal, because I still can't quite believe it), I would not act like a silly fangirl (impossible, as it turns out); instead, I wanted to talk to him about how he dealt with his wife's illness because I wanted to know what it was like for a partner to watch their loved one in pain and how they could support them. One night, we were sitting there in the hotel restaurant, and in walks Rob with Paul Doucette, drummer and guitarist for the band. Holy shit. I was in the same room as Rob Thomas! I felt paralysed. Time for a little pep talk with my guides. 'Come on, Dan, get yourself together; he's just an ordinary bloke ... who happens to be known by millions of people worldwide.' So, when he went to the bar to get a drink, with a bit of encouragement, I did the same. And. Found. Myself. Standing. Right. Next. To. My. Idol. At that moment, I had no voice. It was Rob who spoke first, and not only spoke, but he also touched my wrist! OMG, Rob Thomas was touching my wrist, actually running his fingers over the only tattoo I have—swoon! And then he asked, 'What does that say?' I explained it was Mum's signature and that she had passed away three years earlier. He went on to say that his mother had passed away 4–5 years ago and that his wife had a tattoo on the same wrist in the same spot that stated *BREATHE*. Funnily enough, he then introduced himself, and I returned the courtesy, but I couldn't help but ask, 'How do you deal with your wife's illness?' He studied me for a moment and told me they took it one day at a time.

So, now ask yourself, was that meeting with Rob Thomas just a coincidence, simply a bit of luck, or had I spent over a year programming my subconscious mind, sending thoughts out to the universe that I had to meet him because I had to ask that one question? You can manifest anything you desire when you truly believe something and feel it deep within your soul.

Meditate

Meditation is a fantastic process for clearing the mind to offer clarity; it's like pushing the reset button. I began with ten minutes each morning, which, admittedly, I struggled with, as my brain just would not switch off. I'm not sure I'm much better after only three months into this new ritual, but I'm persevering and learning to change focus when I realise my mind has wandered. Many people around the world practice meditation to increase calmness and relaxation, improve psychological balance, and enhance overall health and wellbeing. Have a look at the Buddhist monks; they are at peace, they speak softly, they don't engage in conflict, and they show appreciation for all that life offers them.

Gratitude

The law of attraction states that the more positive we are and the more grateful we are, the more blessings we will receive. Each morning, I start the day with an affirmation or a gratitude blessing. This could be as simple as stating thanks for enjoying a good night's sleep in a comfortable bed or being able to open your eyes to take in the daybreak. The more we show gratitude, the more blessings we will receive. I have begun writing in a gratitude journal of sorts. It came by way of an exercise from the book, *Ask and It Is Given* that asks readers to begin writing in a notebook titled 'The Book of Positive Aspects'. The premise is that every time you think negatively about an item or situation that you find yourself in, you begin to list everything positive about it. As you think of all the positive aspects, your energy will change from the negative and you will feel better about the situation and your environment in general. More than likely, it will reframe your whole approach to the day.

Give

The message that all the influential motivational speakers continue to repeat is *'Give'*—predominantly money and time. There is nothing more rewarding than helping another less fortunate than yourself, whether that be buying or cooking them a meal, donating money towards a sleeping bag so they are kept warm at night, or spending time with them when they have no-one else. I was a volunteer with the local Apex Club for a few years and thoroughly enjoyed raising funds to send disadvantaged children off to a camp for a week where they could leave their troubles at home and just be kids for a bit. They were taught life skills, they were socialised, and they learned kindness; it was beautiful to watch them evolve as individuals during that week (I was also a 'counsellor' one year, which involved me staying at the camp with the kids from my area). When I was in secondary school, we would spend an afternoon at an aged care facility, talking to the residents and playing cards or bingo. It was a joyous way to give back to the community, and I relished listening to their stories, immersing myself in their world or culture, and seeing life from a different perspective.

Once you begin to complete activities, void of any selfishness or arrogance, the universe rewards you. Yet again we find ourselves following the Law of Attraction—what we put out, we get back—and, by that reasoning, if we are focusing on doing good things for others, we are less likely to focus on our pain and misfortunes.

By now, you should have a basic understanding of how our mindset is crucial to healing and nurturing our bodies. I would love to know about your experiences and whether you continue to seek information about the Law of Attraction after you finish reading this book.

Mindset Action Steps

Step 1—Awaken the Soul

Express gratitude

Seems such a simple task, but many do not express their gratitude for the wonderful blessings in their life. This could be as simple as being thankful that the sun shines on your face or that your legs, which you have often criticised in the past, have managed to keep you upright for another day and allowed you to walk to and from work. And although you are likely to be in some sort of pain or suffering fatigue, the positive of the situation is that you are here to feel that pain or emotion and there is a way forward. I very well could have been dead at the age of seven, or the age of twenty-seven. Despite the pain, I was, and am, grateful to be alive.

Meditate

Now, this doesn't have to be a formal process of sitting down in a quiet space and listening to a meditation; you could simply take five minutes at your desk or in your yard, even in your kitchen, to close your eyes and quieten your mind. This is when we are most connected to Spirit, or God, or whatever you wish to call the spiritual realm.

Complete selfless acts
Unless you are cold-hearted and devoid of emotion, when you do something that benefits another, you can feel your heart swell and your smile widens. Do more of this, more often! Not only are you brightening someone else's day or life, but you are raising your vibrational energy with the universe, which allows more of your dreams to come true.

Step 2—Develop Your Spirituality

Create a vision board or journal
I love this activity. I'm very good at visualising in my mind and I loved being creative when I was younger, but as we get older, I feel we lose that sense of childishness, as society dictates that now we must be mature and responsible. I listened to an interview with Edwina Murphy-Droomer, who leads a workshop called 'Dare to Dream Vision Board', which stirred the creative juices after many dormant years. Before I knew it, I had ordered a beautiful journal from Booktopia and was looking up pictures on the internet of everything that I had ever dreamed about—abundant vegetable gardens, overflowing fruit trees, a busy appointment book, a lady reading this very book, holiday destinations, a black Range Rover (because we

all have to treat ourselves) ... I look at this journal every day, reinforcing the pictures and words in my mind so they become my reality.

Live your dreams

Do not accept others' criticism that you are 'too much of a dreamer'—dream away, for you are creating your reality! We are all capable of manifesting the life we want to live. Many spiritual practitioners believe that to heal the body, one must heal the soul first. Your thoughts and words become your reality; the subconscious mind must be restored with the right ideas. Take my dream of owning a Range Rover as an example. Not only do I have the pictures in my journal and on my whiteboard that I look at every day, but I have visualised the car in my driveway, just as I have visualised driving it. I see Range Rovers everywhere, and the next step is to take one for a test drive. I can see it, I can feel it, and I have put in my order with the universe. I don't need to know how it is going to appear; I only need to believe that it will. As you think, so it shall be—just make sure you're giving the universe the right thoughts and information!

Get in tune with your intuition

We all have an innate intelligence, that angel we feel on our shoulders. When you tune into your intuition and you feel comfortable and at peace, that's the universe telling you it's got your back. Sonia Choquette lists four steps in her book, *Tune In,* that assist readers to tune into their intuition by conducting simple tasks and answering questions designed to get you thinking about what it is you want out of life. Are you following your true purpose by doing what makes your soul sing?

Section 4:

Healthy Habits for Life

I wrote this book to provide those suffering from an autoimmune disease with a solution to their pain in the hope that it may help and that you might join me on my mission to eradicate illness and disease. Yes, it may seem daunting to begin with, but when you begin to see an improvement in symptoms, energy levels, and mental health, you will find the motivation to continue. This protocol is about more than food and toxins; it teaches you to be a critical thinker, develops your research skills, and it encourages you to take responsibility for your health, to not flippantly listen to the medical profession but to listen to your innate intelligence and truly understand what your body needs to function optimally. You are creating healthy habits and instilling this value in family and friends to improve their lives as well; this is a beautiful, selfless act.

I had a friend around for dinner the other night—nothing fancy, just Mexican bowls—and he asked me, 'Do you really enjoy cooking?' The question took me aback at the time, although I'm not sure why. I thought it was obvious, the way I was hurrying around, getting everything organised. However, upon further reflection, I realised I enjoy cooking considerably more than I used to. Preparing and cooking when I was ill was a means to an end; I had to heal my body. Now, I cook to nourish my family and friends while enjoying the social connection that sharing a meal offers. The bonus is that I am also educating them as I work. The beauty of this protocol is that you don't have to deny yourself anything. I still enjoy a glass (or two) of wine, I still enjoy the odd dessert (albeit one made with healthier alternatives), and I still enjoy (and don't feel guilty) taking an hour to myself, relaxing in the bath reading a book. I've done a lot of work to get to where I am, and I've earnt it, but the most uplifting aspect is that I am still here to enjoy it all. I have not allowed my diagnosis to define how I live; in fact, I've crushed my diagnosis, and you can too. It's now time for you to get started; it's time for you to prioritise your health and wellbeing so you can fill from a full cup, giving not only your best to yourself but to your loved ones, work, and social commitments. Go slay those dragons!

Work With Me

There is no-one more qualified to talk about chronic illness than someone who is living or has lived with it. I want to hear what you're experiencing and work with you to unpack the diet and lifestyle factors contributing to your condition. Together, we will tailor an Autoimmune Warrior Protocol package that best suits you and your lifestyle. I was fortunate to have a good friend who supported me through my journey, someone who saw me at my absolute worst and would wait out the pain with me, someone who helped research natural therapies, and someone who would remind me not to give up. Think of me as that person for you! Don't for a minute think that you've been given a life sentence, that you must live with a chronic illness. Having experienced the worst, debilitating pain and fatigue, among other symptoms, and being able to get on top of it and manage it to a point where it no longer affects my daily life, I genuinely believe you can do it too, and I look forward to sharing that journey with you.

STARTUP PROGRAM—budget-friendly alternative to intensive coaching, self-paced, eight weeks, and includes:

- a summary of the Autoimmune Warrior Protocol
- basic education to promote healthier nutrition and lifestyle
- worksheets to complete and hold you to account.

AUTOIMMUNE WARRIOR PROTOCOL—intensive one-on-one coaching, long-term duration (3–12 months), and includes:

- a tailored protocol to reduce symptoms of an autoimmune condition or improve physical/mental disposition
- education that promotes healthier nutrition and lifestyle
- monthly consultations
- regular check-ins.

Connect with Me

Website—www.innatehealthlatrobe.com.au
Facebook—Innate Health Latrobe
Instagram—innatehealth_latrobe
Email—innate.health.latrobe@gmail.com

Bibliography

Alt, M. T. (2016). *The Autoimmune Wellness Handbook.* New York: Rodale.

Ballantyne, S. (2013). *The Paleo Approach.* Canada: Victory Belt Publishing Inc.

Ballantyne, S. (2017). *Paleo Principles.* Canada: Victory Belt Publishing Inc.

DeiCas, M. (2020). Functional Lipids in Autoimmune Inflammatory Diseases. *International Journal of Molecular Science*.

Dormedy, E. (2000). Validation of Acid Washes as Critical Control Points in Hazard Analysis and Critical Point Systems. *Journal of Food Protection*, 1676-1680.

Elkan, A. (2012). Diet nd fatty acid pattern among patients with SLE: associations with disease activity, blood lipids and atherosclerosis. *Lupus*, 1405-1411.

Gedgaudas, N. (2009). *Primal Body, Primal Mind.* Vermont: Healing Arts Press.

Gille, D. (2018). Fermented Food and Non-Communicable Chronic Disease: A Review. *Nutrients*.

Hicks, E. (2006). *The Law of Attraction*. Australia: McPherson's Printing Group.

Humphries, P. (2008). Direct and indirect cellular effects of aspartame on the brain. *European Journal of Clinical Nutrition*, 451-462.

Kummerow, F. (2009). The negative effects of hydrogenated trans fats and what to do about them. *Atherosclerosis*, 458-65.

Laake, I. (2012). Intake of trans fatty acids from partially hydrogenated vegetable and fish oils and ruminant fat in relation to cancer risk. *International Journal of Cancer*, 1389-1403.

Lerner, A. &. (2015). Changes in intestinal tight junction permeability associated with industrial food additives explain the rising incidence of autoimmune disease. *Autoimmunity Reviews*, 479-489.

Liu, Y. (2021). Functional comparison of breast milk, cow milk and goat milk based on changes in the intestinal flora of mice. *LWT*.

Manzel, A. (2014). Role of 'Western Diet' in Inflammatory Autoimmune Diseases. *Current Allergy and Asthma Reports*.

Mercola, J. (2020). *EMF*D*. Australia: Hay House.

Miserandino, C. The Spoon Theory. https://butyoudontlooksick.com/articles/written-by-christine/the-spoon-theory/

Nielsen, M. (2008). *Manifesting Matisse*. USA.

Noble, E. (2017). Gut to Brain Dysbiosis: Mechanisms

Linking Western Diet Consumption, the Microbiome and Cognitive Impairment. *Frontiers in Behavioural Science.*

O'Meara, C. (2019). *Lab to Table.* Australia: Changing Habits.

Seneff, S. (2021). *Toxic Legacy.* United Kingdom: Chelsea Green Publishing.

Williams, A. A. (1954). *Margarine.* London: Pergamon Press Ltd.

Recommended Resources

Nutrition

Books

- *The Paleo Approach & Paleo Principles*—Sarah Ballantyne
- *The Autoimmune Wellness Handbook*—Mickey Trescott and Angie Alt
- *Lab to Table*—Cyndi O'Meara
- *The Autoimmune Fix*—Tom O'Bryan
- *Heal Your Gut*—Lee Holmes
- *The Autoimmune Solution*—Amy Meyers
- *Gap and Psychology/Physiology Syndrome*—Natasha Campbell-McBride
- *The Wahls Protocol*—Terry Wahls
- *The Microbiome Solution*—Robynne Chutkan
- *Primal Body, Primal Mind*—Nora Gedgaudas
- *Deep Nutrition*—Catherine Shanahan.

Documentaries

- *The Magic Pill*—Pete Evans
- *What's With Wheat?*—Cyndi O'Meara
- *That Sugar Film*—Damon Gameau
- *Food, Inc*—Robert Kenner
- *Fed Up*—Stephanie Soechtig
- *Super Size Me*—Morgan Spurlock
- *Fat, Sick, and Nearly Dead*—Joe Cross.

Videos

Any video/interview with Zach Bush—*The Root Cause of Disease and How to Prevent It, How the Microbiome Can Improve Gut Health, Restoring Health, Glyphosate and Healing the Gut.*

Lifestyle

Books

- *Toxic Legacy*—Stephanie Seneff
- *Whitewash*—Carey Gillam
- *Why You Should Give A F*ck About Farming*—Gabrielle Chan
- *EMF*D*—Joseph Mercola
- *The Invisible Rainbow*—Arthur Firstenberg
- *The Healing Power of Essential Oils*—Eric Zielinski
- *The Essential Oils Diet*—Eric and Sabrina Zielinski
- *The Art of Self Love*—Kim Morrison.

Videos
- The Story of Stuff—The Story of Stuff Project, YouTube, <https://www.youtube.com/watch?v=9GorqroigqM>
- The Harmful Effects of Glyphosate—Dr. Stephanie Seneff's presentation on harmful effects of glyphosate, YouTube, <https://www.youtube.com/watch?v=MqWwhggnbyw>
- Restoring Health, Glyphosate, and Healing the Gut | ZACH BUSH, M.D. | Positive University—Zach Bush, YouTube, <https://www.youtube.com/watch?v=4tBTv0I5-qk>.

Mindset

Books
- *Manifesting Matisse*—Dr Michelle K Nielsen
- *The Law of Attraction series*—Esther and Jerry Hicks
- *The Secret*—Rhonda Byrne
- *The Artist's Way*—Julia Cameron
- *Your Heart's Desire*—Sonia Choquette
- *Tune In*—Sonia Choquette
- *Ask Your Guides*—Sonia Choquette
- *The Psychic Pathway*—Sonia Choquette
- *The Course in Miracles*—Pam Grout
- *Thank and Grow Rich*—Pam Grout
- *Abundance*—Deepak Chopra
- *The Art of Living*—Thich Nhat Hanh

- *The Miracle of Mindfulness*—Thich Nhat Hanh
- *The Game of Life and How to Play It*—Florence Scovel Shinn.

Documentaries
- *The Secret*—Netflix.

Acknowledgements

Just as it takes a village to raise a child, it takes a village to help a loved one overcome their health battle—and publish a book about it, no less!

To my partner, Trevor, who came into my life after I had gone through the worst and now gets me at my best: what a lucky guy you are! You have stood by me through all my hare-brained schemes and ideas when others would have run. Thank you for allowing me to spread my wings and not push you away.

To my friend (and former boss), Michael Alexander, who was there from diagnosis and provided unwavering support during the years I was in incredible pain; I will be eternally grateful for the time you gave to me, even if it meant watching *Gossip Girl* and straightening my hair, and for the moments you recognised the internal battle that was taking place and allowed me to rest.

To my friends who are family by choice: the Hardys (Gav, Stace, Mike, and Taylah), Mum (Julie Whitmore), Ryan Whitmore, Kerrie Phillips, Shane Leinberger, and

Belinda Cantwell. The world is a brighter place with you in it; thank you for allowing me into your lives and for keeping me sane when it all became a tad overwhelming.

To Marion and Brian Phillips, thank you for accepting to adopt me into your family at the ripe old age of thirty-eight.

To everyone who has watched me grow over the last forty years and now chuckles at the fact that I am following in my parents' footsteps: never underestimate how much of an impact you have on someone's life, even if you don't see each other often.

To all the healthcare professionals who came before me and have spent tireless hours and years researching and dedicating their lives to the prevention of illness and disease: the information you provided is, and will continue, to help so many other sufferers of autoimmune afflictions— together, we can eradicate illness and disease!

To the team at Ocean Reeve Publishing: thank you for your support and mentoring in bringing my dream to fruition. Next time, I might try my hand at fiction …

To anyone who has picked up this book. It is my sincerest wish that you can take something from my experience and apply it to your situation. Thank you for reading; it is your support that keeps me doing the work I am passionate about.